GEMSTONE
BUYING GUIDE

GEMSTONE
BUYING GUIDE

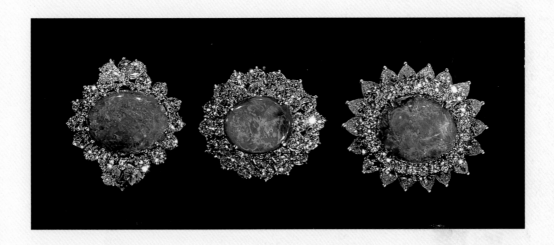

Renée Newman

International Jewelry Publications
Los Angeles _____

This publication is designed to provide information in regard to the subject matter covered. It is sold with the understanding that the publisher and author are not engaged in rendering legal, financial, or other professional services. If legal or other expert assistance is required, the services of a competent professional should be sought. International Jewelry Publications and the author shall have neither liability nor responsibility to any person or entity with respect to any loss or damage caused or alleged to be caused directly or indirectly by the information contained in this book. All inquiries should be directed to:

International Jewelry Publications
P.O. Box 13384
Los Angeles, CA 90013-0384 USA

(Inquiries should be accompanied by a self-addressed, stamped envelope.)

Printed in Singapore

Library of Congress Cataloging-in-Publication Data

Newman, Renée.
    Gemstone buying guide / Renée Newman
        p.   cm.
    Includes bibliographical references and index.
    ISBN 0-929975-25-1
    1. Precious stones--Purchasing.   I. Title
TS752.N48   1998
736'.2'0297--dc21   97-24288
                                           CIP

Cover photo: Colored gemstone suite from Cynthia Renée Co.; photography by Robert Weldon.

Half-title page photo: 71.37-carat citrine arrowhead concave faceted by Mark Gronlund; photography by Renée Newman.

Title page photo: Three black opals with unusually fine color. Jewelry from Port Royal Antique Jewelry; photography by Harold & Erica Van Pelt.

Contents

Acknowledgments

I would like to express my appreciation to the following people for their contribution to the *Gemstone Buying Guide*:

Ernie and Regina Goldberger of the Josam Diamond Trading Corporation. This book could never have been written without the experience and knowledge I gained from working with them.

The American Gemological Laboratories and the Gemological Institute of America. They have contributed diagrams and information.

Arthur Anderson, Charles Carmona, Dr. Paul Downing, Pete Flusser, Si and Ann Frazier, Mark Gronlund, Don Kay, Dr. Horst Krupp, Glenn Lehrer, Gail Levine, Peter Malnekoff, Cynthia Marcusson, Dr. Kurt Nassau, Howard Rubin, Sindi Schloss, Sherris Cottier Shank, Gerald Stockton and John S. White. They have made valuable suggestions, corrections and comments regarding the portions of the book they examined. They are not responsible for any possible errors, nor do they necessarily endorse the material contained in this book.

Arthur Anderson, Asian Institute of Gemological Sciences, Color Masters Gem Corp, William Cox, Peggy Croft, Cynthia Renée Co., The Diamond Dove, Inc., Gary Dulac Goldsmith, Stephen Greenstein, Richard Kimball, Glenn Lehrer Designs, Majestic Opals, Mason-Kay, Inc., Dan Miller, Murphy Design, Port Royal Antique Jewelry, Proprioro, Linda Quinn, Rox Designs, Sherris Cottier Shank, Libby Skamfer, Somos Creations, Wearable Sculpture by Trisko, Robert Weldon and Harry Winston Inc. Photos from them have been reproduced in this book.

Manoel Bernardes Ltd., Pete & Bobbi Flusser, Carrie Ginsburg Fine Gems, Mark Gronlund, Josam Diamond Trading Corporation, Danny & Ronny Levy Fine Gems, Overland Gems, Inc., Radiance International, Andrew Sarosi, Gerald Stockton, Timeless Gem Designs, Varna Platinum. Their stones or jewelry have been used for some of the photographs.

Ian & Amy Itescu and Donald Nelson. They have provided technical assistance.

Louise Harris Berlin. She has spent hours carefully editing the *Gemstone Buying Guide*. Thanks to her, this book is much easier for consumers to read and understand.

My sincere thanks to all of these contributors for their kindness and help.

Suppliers of Jewelry & Stones for Photographs

COVER PHOTO: Cynthia Renée Co., Fallbrook, CA

HALF TITLE PAGE PHOTO: Mark Gronlund Custom Jewelry Shop, Enterprise, FL

TITLE PAGE PHOTO: Port Royal Antique Jewelry, Naples, FL

CHAPTER 2

Figs. 2.1, 2.2 & 2.12 Josam Diamond Trading Corporation, Los Angeles, CA
Fig. 2.5 Richard H. Kimball Designs, Inc., Denver, CO
Figs. 2.6, 2.14, 2.31 & 2.38 Cynthia Renée Co., Fallbrook, CA
Fig. 2.9 Color Masters Gem Corp., New York, NY
Fig. 2.10 Harry Winston, Inc., New York, NY
Fig. 2.13 Proprioro, San Francisco, CA
Fig. 2.18 Mason-Kay, Inc., Denver, CO
Fig. 2.19 Timeless Gem Designs, Los Angeles, CA
Fig. 2.20 The Diamond Dove, Inc., Boulder, CO
Figs. 2.21 & 2.22 Gemscapes Sculptured Gemstones, Southfield, MI
Fig. 2.23 Gary Dulac Goldsmith, Inc., Vero Beach, FL
Figs. 2.24 to 2.28 & 2.37 Glenn Lehrer Designs, San Rafael, CA
Fig. 2.29 Somos Creations, Valley Cottage, NY
Fig. 2.30 William Cox Gem Carvings, Provo, UT
Figs. 2.32 to 2.34 Mark Gronlund Custom Jewelry Shop, Enterprise, FL
Fig. 2.35 Speira Gems, Ashland, OR
Fig. 2.39 Carrie G. (Carrie Ginsburg Fine Gemstones), Los Angeles, CA
Fig 2.40 Stephen Greenstein Design, Montaud, France

CHAPTER 4

Fig. 4.1 American Gemological Laboratories, New York, NY
Fig. 4.2 Color Masters Gem Corp, New York, NY
Figs. 4.3 & 4.5 Harry Winston, Inc., New York, NY
Fig. 4.4 Carrie G., Los Angeles, CA

CHAPTER 5

Figs. 5.1 to 5.3, 5.5 & 5.6 Overland Gems, Los Angeles, CA
Figs. 5.7 & 5.8 Danny & Ronny Levy Fine Gems, Los Angeles, CA

CHAPTER 6

Fig. 6.1 Overland Gems, Los Angeles, CA
Fig. 6.4 Carrie G., Los Angeles, CA
Figs. 6.7 & 6.8 Josam Diamond Trading Corporation, Los Angeles, CA
Fig. 6.10 Mark Gronlund Custom Jewelry Shop, Enterprise, FL
Fig. 6.11 Glenn Lehrer Designs, San Rafael, CA

CHAPTER 7

Figs. 7.1 to 7.3 Andrew Sarosi, Los Angeles, CA
Fig. 7.5 Danny & Ronny Levy Fine Gems, Los Angeles, CA

CHAPTER 11

Figs. Al.1 to Al.3 Andrew Sarosi, Los Angeles, CA
Fig. Al.4 Carrie G., Los Angeles, CA
Fig. Am.1 Cynthia Renée Co., Fallbrook, CA
Fig. Am.2 Peggy Croft Wax Sculpturing, Los Angeles, CA
Figs. Am.3 & Am.8 Linda K. Quinn Designs, Strafford, MO
Fig. Am.4 Timeless Gem Designs, Los Angeles, CA
Fig. Am.5 The Diamond Dove, Inc., Boulder, CO
Fig. Am.7 Somos Creations, Valley Cottage, NY
Fig. Ca.1 William Cox Gem Carvings, Provo, UT
Figs. Ca.2 & Ca.8 Richard H. Kimball Designs, Inc., Denver, CO
Fig. Ca.4 & Ca.9 Timeless Gem Designs, Los Angeles, CA
Figs. Ca.10 & Ca.11 Murphy Design, Minneapolis, MN
Fig. Em.1 Gemscapes Sculptured Gemstones, Southfield, MI
Fig. Em.2 Color Masters Gem Corp, New York, NY
Fig. Em.3 Robert Trisko Jewelry Sculptures, Waite Park, MN
Fig. Em.4 Cynthia Renée Co., Fallbrook, CA
Fig. Em.5 Glenn Lehrer Designs, San Rafael, CA
Fig. Em.6 Harry Winston, Inc., New York, NY
Fig. Em.7 Carrie G., Los Angeles, CA
Fig. G.1 Cynthia Renée Co., Fallbrook, CA
Fig. G.2 Gary Dulac Goldsmith, Inc., Vero Beach, FL
Fig. G.3 Libby Skamfer, Chicago, IL
Fig. G.4 Linda K. Quinn Designs, Strafford, MO
Fig. G.5 Carrie G., Los Angeles, CA
Fig. G.6 Dan Miller Jewelry, Laguna Beach, CA
Fig. G.7 and I.1 Proprioro, San Francisco, CA
Figs. J.1 to J.6 & J.8 to J.11, Mason-Kay, Denver, CO
Fig. L.1 Gerald Stockton, Inc., Los Angeles, CA

Fig. L.2 Richard H. Kimball Designs, Inc., Denver, CO
Fig. Ma.2 Murphy Design, Minneapolis, MN
Fig. Fe.1 Timeless Gem Designs, Los Angeles, CA
Fig. Fe.5 Carrie G., Los Angeles, CA
Fig. Op.1 Majestic Opals, Inc., Estes, Park, CO
Figs. Op.2, Op.4, Op.10, Op.11, & Op.13 Port Royal Antique Jewelry, Naples, FL
Fig. Op.3 & Op.8 Rox Designs, Chicago, IL
Figs. Op.5 & Op.7 Gerald Stockton, Inc., Los Angeles, CA
Fig. Op.9 The Diamond Dove, Inc., Boulder, CO
Fig. Op.12 Proprioro, San Francisco, CA
Figs. Op.17 to Op.19, Op. 21 & Op.22 Port Royal Antique Jewelry, Naples, FL
Fig. P.1 Timeless Gem Designs, Los Angeles, CA
Fig. P.2 Varna Platinum, Los Angeles, CA
Fig Sp.2 Overland Gems, Los Angeles, CA
Fig. RS.1 Harry Winston, Inc., Los Angeles, CA
Fig. RS.2 Color Masters Gem Corp, New York, NY
Fig. RS.3 Cynthia Renée Co., Fallbrook, CA
Fig. RS.4 Asian Institute of Gemological Sciences, Bangkok, Thailand
Fig. RS.5 Radiance International, San Diego, CA
Figs. S.1, S.3 & S.5, Cynthia Renée Co., Fallbrook, CA
Fig. S.2 Gary Dulac Goldsmith, Inc., Vero Beach, FL
Fig. S.4 Linda K. Quinn Designs, Strafford, MO
Fig. Tz.1 Carrie G., Los Angeles, CA
Fig. Tz.3 Robert Trisko Jewelry Sculptures, Waite Park, MN
Fig. Tz.4 Proprioro, San Francisco, CA
Fig. Tp.1 Linda K. Quinn Designs, Strafford, MO
Figs. Tp.2 & Tp.3, Cynthia Renée Co., Fallbrook, CA
Fig. Tp.4 Manoel Bernardes Ltd., Belo Horizonte, Minas Gerais, Brazil
Figs. Tm.1 & Tm.3 Richard H. Kimball Designs, Inc., Denver, CO
Figs. Tm.2 & Tm.11 Linda K. Quinn Designs, Strafford, MO
Figs. Tm.4 & Tm.10 Cynthia Renée Co., Fallbrook, CA
Fig. Tm.5 Timeless Gem Designs, Los Angeles, CA
Fig. Tm.7 Dan MIller Jewelry, Laguna Beach, CA
Fig. Tm.8 Gary Dulac Goldsmith, Inc., Vero Beach, FL
Fig. Tm.9 Carrie G., Los Angeles, CA
Fig. Tq.1 Timeless Gem Designs, Los Angeles, CA
Fig. Tq.2 Richard H. Kimball Designs, Inc., Denver, CO
Figs. Z.1 & Z.4 Cynthia Renée Co., Fallbrook, CA
Fig. Z.2 Timeless Gem Designs, Los Angeles, CA
Fig. Z.3 Overland Gems, Los Angeles, CA

1

Why Read a Whole Book
Just to Buy a Gemstone?

Suppose you want to get an opal for someone special. If you try to buy one without some background knowledge, you might end up with a milky white opal with little play of color. Some jewelry stores only stock this type because it's cheap and available in mass quantities. Milky opal is acceptable if you're looking for a white, low-priced stone, but it's not appropriate for a special gift.

Even if you find a good selection of opals, you'll need information about their quality; but that could be hard to obtain in a jewelry store. The salespeople may not know much about opals; sales tags and sales receipts don't tell you anything about quality; and it's not feasible to take every opal that interests you to an appraiser before you buy it. If you want to get good buys on opals and make wise choices, you must become an educated buyer, Brochures or books on opal lore, history, mining and sources won't be of much help. You need information that tells you how to evaluate opals. The *Gemstone Buying Guide* is a good introduction to analyzing the quality of opals and other colored gems.

Naturally, you'll need professional assistance when you make your gem purchases. The knowledge you gain from this book will make it easier for you to select a good jeweler. You will learn far more about jewelers by examining their merchandise and discussing it with them than by asking questions such as "How long have you been in business?" "Where were you trained?" "What trade organizations do you belong to?" The answers can be fabricated, and they aren't always a true indication of the jeweler's knowledge, skill or ethics. Therefore, it's important for you to be informed about gems. A book on judging gem quality can help you determine if a salesperson is knowledgeable and interested in your welfare.

Even when you deal with competent jewelers, it's impossible for them to discuss thoroughly the pricing and evaluation of colored stones during a brief visit to their store. It would be better to first learn some fundamental information by reading this book. Instead of spending time on basics, jewelers can show you how to apply your new-found knowledge when selecting stones, and they can help you find what you want. A prior knowledge of gems will also help you understand and retain what a jeweler tells you.

What This Book Is Not

♦ It's not a guide to making a fortune on buying and selling gems. Nobody can guarantee that a gem will increase in value and that it can be resold for more than its retail cost. However, understanding the value concepts discussed in this book can increase your chances of finding good buys on gemstones.

♦ It's not a ten-minute guide to appraising gemstones. There's a lot to learn before being able to accurately compare gems for value. That's why a book is needed on the subject. The *Gemstone Buying Guide* is just an introduction, but it does have enough information to give laypeople a good background for understanding price differences.

♦ It's not a scientific treatise on the chemistry, crystallography and geological distribution of gemstones. The material in this book, however, is based on technical research. Chapter 11 lists physical and optical properties of the most important colored stones to help you identify them. Technical terms needed for buying or grading gems are explained in everyday language.

♦ It's not a discussion about the mining and prospecting of gemstones. You don't need to know how to mine a gem to buy one. If you're interested in good references on gem mining and sources, some are listed in the bibliography.

♦ It's not a substitute for examining actual stones. Photographs do not accurately reproduce color, nor do they show the three-dimensional nature of gemstones very well. Concepts such as brilliancy and transparency are best understood when looking at real stones.

♦ It's not s *complete* guide to buying gems. No book can tell you everything you need to know to buy a gemstone, not even more specialized books such as the *Emerald & Tanzanite Buying Guide* by the same author. The goal of the *Gemstone Buying Guide* is to provide fundamentals on evaluating the quality of important colored stones. Many gemstones are not included. For information on judging diamond quality, consult the *Diamond Ring Buying Guide*.

What This Book Is

♦ A guide to evaluating the quality of colored gemstones.

♦ An aid to avoiding fraud with information on imitations, synthetics and treatments.

♦ A handy reference on colored stones for laypeople and professionals.

♦ A collection of practical tips on choosing and caring for gems.

♦ A challenge to view colored stones through the eyes of gemologists and gem dealers.

How to Use This Book

The *Gemstone Buying Guide* is not meant to be read like a murder mystery or a science fiction thriller. If you're new to the study of gems, you may find this book overwhelming at first. So start by looking at the pictures and by reading the Table of Contents. Then learn the basic terminology in Chapter 2 and continue slowly, perhaps a chapter at a time.

Skip over any sections that don't interest you or that are too complicated. This book has far more information than the average person will care to learn. That's because it's also designed to be a reference. When questions arise about colored gems, you can avoid lengthy research by having many of the answers right at your fingertips.

To get the most out of the *Gemstone Buying Guide*, you should try to actively use what you learn. Buy or borrow a loupe (jeweler's magnifying glass) and start examining any jewelry you might have at home. Look around in jewelry stores and ask the professionals there to show you different qualities and varieties of the gems that interest you. If you have appraisals or grading reports, study them carefully. If there's something you don't understand, ask for an explanation.

Shopping for gemstones should not be a chore. It should be fun. There is no fun, though, in worrying about being deceived or in buying a stone that turns out to be a poor choice. Use this book to gain the knowledge, confidence and independence you need to select the stones that are best for you. Use it also to gain a greater appreciation for the jewelry you already own. Buying gemstones represents a significant investment of time and money. Let the *Gemstone Buying Guide* help make this investment a pleasurable and rewarding experience.

2

Shape & Cutting Style

When gemologists speak of a gem's *shape*, they usually mean its face-up outline. The most common gemstone shapes include the round, oval, square, triangle, pear, marquise, heart and **cushion**, a squarish or rectangular shape with curved sides and rounded corners. Gems can be any geometric shape or they may resemble things such as animals, bells, stars, the moon, etc. They can also be cut as abstract freeforms. Gem cutters try to select shapes and cutting styles which allow them to emphasize preferred colors and brilliance, minimize undesirable flaws, and/or get the maximum weight yield from the rough. In small calibrated sizes, there is a tendency to cut what jewelry manufacturers want, even when some shapes cause a greater weight loss. Standard sizes and shapes are required for mass-produced jewelry.

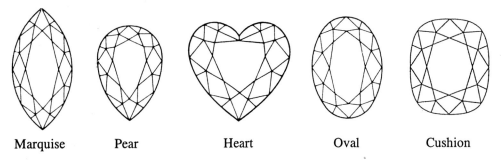

Marquise   Pear   Heart   Oval   Cushion

Cutting style refers to the way in which a stone is cut or faceted. An oval-shaped stone, for example, may just be rounded as a cabochon or it may have facets (polished surfaces with varying shapes) that are arranged in different styles. The term *emerald cut* has a double meaning. It indicates that the shape is square or rectangular with clipped-off corners and that the faceting style is a step cut, which has parallel rows of long, four-sided facets. A **radiant cut** has the same shape as an emerald cut but has facets similar to those of a round brilliant cut.

Fig. 2.1 Emerald cut

Fig. 2.2 Radiant cut

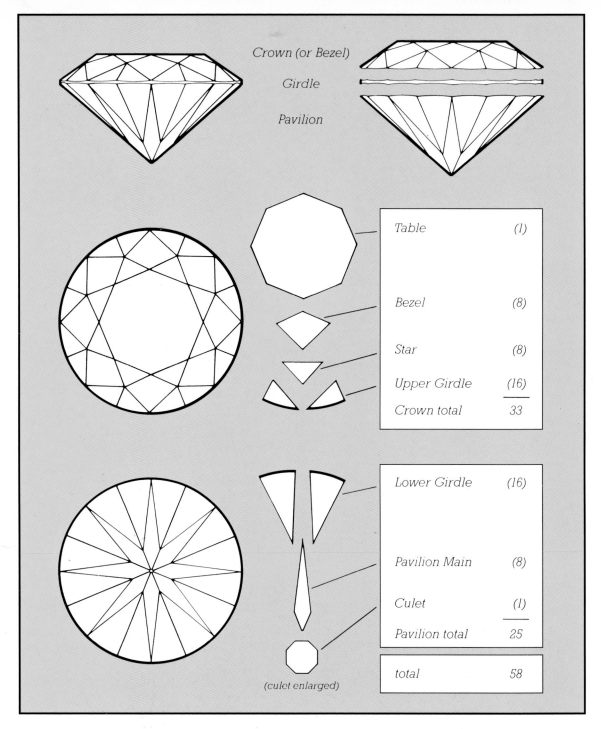

Fig. 2.3 Facet arrangement of a standard round brilliant cut. *Diagram reprinted with permission from the Gemological Institute of America.*

Sometimes rough gem material is not cut into any particular shape. Instead, it is just rounded and polished leaving the basic shape of the rough intact. This process is called **tumbling** and is generally used when the material doesn't warrant cutting. The rough pieces are tumbled in a rotating barrel with abrasives and water. As the stones slide against each other, they become smooth like pebbles in rivers that rub against sand and other pebbles. Tumbling is the simplest technique for fashioning gem rough. The resulting shape is described as **baroque**, which means "irregular in outline."

Gemstone Terms Defined

To help you understand the sections on cutting styles, here are some basic terms:

Facets   The polished surfaces or planes on a stone. Normally they are flat, but some cutters are now creating stones with concave facets. Facets are intended to create brilliance in a gemstone.

Table   The large, flat top facet. It normally has an octagonal shape on a round stone.

Girdle   The narrow rim around the stone. The girdle plane is parallel to the table and is the largest diameter of any part of the stone.

Crown   The upper part of the stone above the girdle.

Pavilion   The lower part of the stone below the girdle.

Culet   The tiny facet on the pointed bottom of the pavilion, parallel to the table. Sometimes the point of a stone is called "the culet" even if no culet facet is present.

Fancy Shape   Any shape except round. This term is most frequently applied to diamonds.

Traditional Cutting Styles

Before the 1300's, gems were usually cut into unfaceted rounded beads or into cabochons (unfaceted dome-shaped stones). Colored gems looked attractive cut this way, but diamonds looked dull. Thanks to man's interest in bringing out the beauty of diamonds, the art of faceting gemstones was developed. At first, facets were added haphazardly, but by around 1450, diamonds began to be cut with a symmetrical

Fig. 2.4 Table cut

arrangement of facets. The first symmetrical style probably evolved out of the natural octahedral shape of some diamond crystals. Simply by flattening one point or cutting it off, a table facet was formed. This created a symmetrical style called the **table cut**, which had a crown, pavilion and nine facets (ten if there were a culet). More complex styles gradually emerged, and there were advances in cutting tools and technology. One of the most important developments was the introduction of the rotary diamond saw around 1900. By the 1920's, the modern round-brilliant cut had become popular.

As cutters discovered how faceting could bring out the brilliance and sparkle of diamonds, they started to apply the same techniques to colored stones. Today, gems are cut into the following basic styles:

Cabochon Cut   Has a dome-shaped top and either a flat or rounded bottom. This is the simplest cut for a stone and is often seen in antique jewelry. Today this cutting style tends to be used for opaque, translucent, and star or cat's-eye stones. but transparent material is also used. Sometimes stones are cut as a cabochon on top and faceted on the bottom to add some brilliance.

Cabochon

Since the **cabochon** is the simplest style, it costs less to cut than faceted styles. Another reason cabochons are generally priced less is that they are often made from lower quality material that is unsuitable for faceting. Cabochon stones can also be of high quality, especially those found in antique jewelry.

Fig. 2.5 Green tourmaline cabochon with a textured base. *Ring by Richard Kimball; photo by Steve Ramsey.*

Fig. 2.6 A full pear-shaped tourmaline cabochon forms the amphora base. *Jewelry from Cynthia Renée Co.; photo by Robert Weldon.*

Step Cut   Has rows of facets that resemble the steps of a staircase. The facets are usually four-sided and elongated, and parallel to the girdle. One example is the **baguette**, a square-cornered, rectangular stone. If step-cuts have clipped-off corners, they're called **emerald cuts** because emeralds are often cut this way. This protects the corners and provides places where prongs can secure the stone. Emerald-cut stones tend to have more facets than baguettes. They are usually rectangular or square, but they can also be triangular.

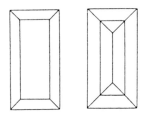

Fig. 2.7 Step-cut baguette

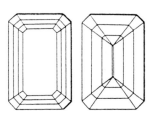

Fig. 2.8 Emerald cut

Fig. 2.9 Emerald-cut sapphire surrounded by diamond baguettes. *Ring and photo courtesy Color Masters Gem Corp.*

Fig. 2.10 Emerald tapered baguettes around a brilliant-cut heart-shape diamond. *Jewelry and photo courtesy Harry Winston, Inc.*

Brilliant Cut

Has mostly 3-sided facets which radiate outward from the stone. Kite- or lozenge-shaped facets may also be present. The best-known example is the **full-cut round brilliant**, which has 58 facets. Ovals, pears, marquises, and heart-shapes can also be brilliant-cut. The **single cut**, which has 17 or 18 facets, is another type of brilliant cut.

Fig. 2.11 Single cut

It may be found on small stones, often of low quality, or on imitations. Square stones cut in the brilliant style are called **princess cuts**. Triangular brilliant cuts are called **trilliants**. The princess and trilliant cuts were originally developed for diamonds because their brilliant-style facets create a greater amount of brilliance and sparkle than step facets do. Now the princess and trilliant cuts are becoming popular for colored stones.

Gemstone pendants or earrings are occasionally cut as **briolettes**. These have a tear-drop shape, a circular cross-section and brilliant-style facets (or occasionally rectangular, step-cut-style facets or else no facets).

Fig. 2.12 Princess cut

Fig. 2.13 Tanzanite trilliant. *Ring courtesy of Proprioro; photo by TKO Studios.*

Fig. 2.14 Ametrine briolette from Cynthia Renée Co. *Photo by Colladay.*

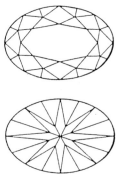

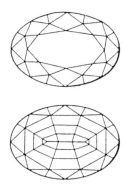

Fig. 2.15 Brilliant cut   Fig. 2.16 Mixed cut

Mixed cut   Has both step- and brilliant-cut facets.   This is a popular faceting style for colored stones.   The crown is brilliant-cut to maximize brilliance and hide flaws if present.   The pavilion, on the other hand, is either entirely step cut or else has a combination of both step- and brilliant-type facets.   The step facets allow cutters to save weight and bring out the color of the stone.   Occasionally, the mixed cut is referred to as the **Ceylon cut**.

Bead (faceted & unfaceted)   Usually has a ball-shaped form with a hole through the center.   Most faceted beads have either brilliant- or step-type facets.   Today, beads are generally made from lower-priced material.   High-quality rubies and emeralds, for example, are usually faceted.   It would be pointless to lower their weight and value by drilling holes through them.

Fig. 2.17 Step-cut bead

Fig. 2.18 Black jade beads, bangle and figurine. *Photo and jewelry courtesy Mason-Kay.*

Carving

Carving is a specialized type of cutting which produces intricate designs and forms, not just flat facets or evenly curved surfaces. Any of the following art forms can be considered a carving:

Engraving: A shallow design cut into the surface of a stone. The overall shape and contour of the stone is changed very little.

Cameo: A stone, often banded chalcedony, with a design or picture cut in relief. The background is removed to expose the desired picture.

Intaglio: An engraved stone with a design cut shallow into its surface.

Sculpture: Stone cut as a three-dimensional object such as a figurine or bust.

Three-dimensional gemstone carving, also called loosely in the trade a **fantasy cut:** A stone with carved areas that may have some of the same characteristics as a traditional cut—it may be partially faceted or cabbed, and it may have a crown, girdle and pavilion. Gemstone carvers and faceters have similar goals—to bring out the brilliance and color of a gem. However, instead of just using small flat planes to accomplish this, gem carvers may also use grooves, curved planes, recessed areas and undercutting, which create a wide variety of effects.

In the past half century, many talented artists have become involved in gemstone carving because it offers the opportunity to work in a sculptural manner with beautiful color and fascinating optics. As a result, there are many new styles of cutting. Some modern carvers may cut a deep three-dimensional pattern into a stone with a crown, girdle and/or pavilion. The depth of cutting creates a play of light that is as important as the carving pattern itself. Some cutters may concentrate primarily on optical effects and others may depart entirely from recognized gemstone shapes, creating a gem that is entirely free-form.

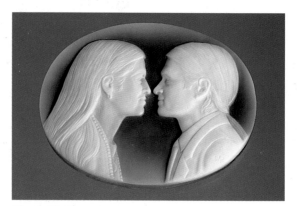

Fig. 2.19 Cameo

Fig. 2.20 Fantasy-cut pink tourmaline by Bernd Munsteiner. *Ring designed, made and photographed by The Diamond Dove, Inc.*

Carvings are usually priced per piece instead of per carat. Their value depends on the skill and fame of the cutter, the type of material used, the time required to execute the design, the fame of their owner(s), and their antique value if any. Custom-crafted, one-of-a-kind designs are naturally more expensive than those which are mass produced or machine-made.

Fig. 2.21 Amethyst sculpted by Sherris Cottier Shank. It is designed to be set in jewelry. *Photo by John McMartin.*

Fig. 2.22 Free-form aquamarine sculpture with 3-dimensional carving. *Designed and sculpted by Sherris Cottier Shank; photo by John McMartin.*

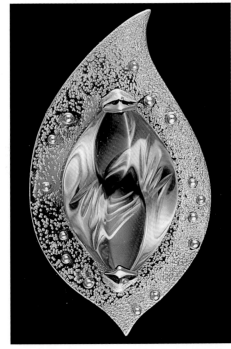

Fig. 2.23 Fantasy-cut citrine in pendant by Gary Dulac. *Photo copyright 1995 by Azad.*

Fig. 2.24 Dendritic agate carved by Glenn Lehrer. *Photo by Azad.*

Fig. 2.25 Brazilian orange drusy agate with diamonds and a South Sea pearl. *Carved and photographed by Glenn Lehrer.*

Fig. 2.26 Chrysocolla carving by Glenn Lehrer, *Photo G. Lehrer.*

Fig. 2.27 Carnelian drusy agate. *Carved and photographed by Glenn Lehrer.*

Fig. 2.28 A carving from a single piece of drusy agate that is half stained and half natural color. *Carved and photographed by Glenn Lehrer.*

Fig. 2.29 Fantasy-cut blue topaz. *Pendant & photo by Somos Creations.*

Fig. 2.30 Carved Oregon sunstone. *Carving and photo courtesy William Cox Gem Carvings.*

Fig. 2.31 Fantasy-cut ametrine brooch. *Jewelry by Cynthia Renée Co. Photo by Colladay.*

Non-traditional Cutting Styles, Variations & Techniques

Concave Faceting Traditionally, the facets on gems have been flat. In recent years, some gem cutters have been experimenting with concave facets. By using concave shapes, faceters can create scalloped girdle outlines and increase brilliance. If light enters a gem and hits a flat facet, it is reflected in one direction. However, if it hits a curved surface, it is scattered in many directions, thereby magnifying the brilliance of the stone. Concave faceting normally takes about two to five times longer than conventional faceting. Consequently, stones with concave facets usually cost more than traditional cuts. Currently the supply of concave-faceted stones is limited.

Fig. 2.32 Two citrines and one amethyst with concave faceting by Mark Gronlund

Fig. 2.33 Citrine arrowhead concave faceted by Mark Gronlund

Fig. 2.34 Back view of arrowhead in figure 2.33

Combination Cuts   Sometimes a gem is both faceted and carved. In the previous section this was referred to as a "gemstone carving." The result is a stone unlike anything normally sold in jewelry stores.

Open Tables   This concept eliminates the crown and spreads the table so that the observer's eye is drawn into the interior of the stone. Both curved and flat facets may be used on the pavilion to create unusual patterns and optical effects when the stone is viewed face up. The "halo cut" in figure 2.35 is an example of this.

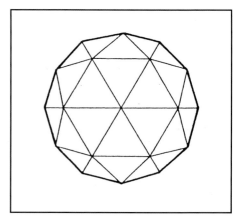

Fig. 2.36 Rose cut

Fig. 2.35 An 8.78-ct golden beryl with an open table "halo" cut by Arthur Lee Anderson. This stone is in the collection of the Smithsonian Institution. *Photo by Robert Jaffe.*

No Tables   Traditional step- and brilliant-cut stones have a large table facet on the crown. Contemporary cutters sometimes eliminate the table. They may facet squares or rectangles of similar size across the crown. This is called a **checkerboard cut** or **opposed-bar cut**, depending on the style. Another example of a faceting style without a table is the old-style **rose cut**, which has triangular brilliant-style facets, a dome-shaped crown, a flat base and a round girdle outline. The **rose cut** may have originated in India and probably dates back to the fifteenth century.

Fig. 2.37 Ring shaped amethyst, citrine, peridot and garnet (torus rings™) carved by Glenn Lehrer. Torus rings™ have no table facet and are designed to be set with a contrasting stone. *Photo by Azad.*

Fig. 2.38 Rectangular facets across the crown of a tourmaline. *Ring from the Cynthia Renée Co.; photo by Robert Weldon.*

Fig. 2.39 Yellow beryl with square facets across the crown (checkerboard cut)

Cutters may also eliminate the concept of a pavilion and a crown and facet both the top and the bottom of the stone in a similar manner.

Textured Surfaces   Instead of having a high polish on all the surfaces of a gem, cutters may texturize some of them. Occasionally rough areas are left on the pavilion to produce interesting designs when the stone is viewed face up.

Fig. 2.40 Aquamarine with a textured base. *Ring by Stephen Greenstein; photo by Frédéric Jauimes.*

Today, cutters are more creative than ever. They are taking low-priced gem material such as quartz, chalcedony and blue topaz and turning it into spectacular works of art. Thanks to the greater emphasis on high-quality cutting, it's easier to find stones with pizazz than it was twenty years ago. For a better idea of what types of styles are now available, go to your local jeweler and ask to see some of the contemporary cuts. Don't forget your wallet. When you see how pretty these gems are, you'll want to own one.

3

Carat Weight

The term "carat" originated in ancient times when gemstones were weighed against the carob bean. Each bean weighed about one carat. Gem traders were aware, though, that the weights varied slightly. This made it advantageous for them to own both "buying" beans and "selling" beans.

In 1913, carat weight was standardized internationally and adapted to the metric system, with one carat equalling 1/5 of a gram. The term "carat" sounds more impressive and is easier to use than fractions of grams. Consequently, it is the preferred unit of weight for gemstones.

The weight of small stones is frequently expressed in **points**, with one point equaling 0.01 carats. For example, five points is the same as five one-hundredths of a carat. Contrary to popular belief, jewelers do not use "point" to refer to the number of facets on a stone. The following chart gives examples of written and spoken forms of carat weight:

Table 3.1

Written	Spoken
0.005 ct (0.5 pt)	half point
0.05 ct	five points
0.25 ct	twenty-five points or a quarter carat
0.50 ct	fifty points or a half carat
1.82 cts	one point eight two (carats) or one eighty-two

Note that "point" when used in expressing weights over one carat refers to the decimal point, not a unit of measure. Also note that "pt" can be used instead of "ct" to make people think for example, that a stone weighs 1/2 carat instead 1/2 of a point.

31

Effect of Carat Weight on Price

Most people are familiar with the principle, the higher the carat weight, the greater the value. However, they may not realize that a one-carat ruby, for example, is worth far more than several small rubies of similar quality with a total weight of one carat. This is because the supply of large rubies is more limited. So when you compare jewelry prices, besides noting the quality, you should pay attention to individual stone weights and **notice the difference between** the labels **1 ct TW** (one carat total weight) **and 1 ct** (the weight of one stone).

When comparing the cost of transparent gems, you should also start noting the **per-carat cost** instead of concentrating on the total cost of the stone. This makes it easier to compare prices more accurately, which is why dealers buy and sell most gems using per-carat prices. However, many opaque and translucent stones such as jade, malachite and chalcedony are sold by the stone or piece, not by weight. Designer cuts may also be priced per piece, and colored stones under about a half carat are often priced according to millimeter size. The following equations will help you calculate the per-carat cost and total cost of gemstones.

$$\text{Per-carat cost} = \frac{\text{stone cost}}{\text{carat weight}}$$

$$\text{Total cost of a stone} = \text{carat weight} \ \text{x} \ \text{per-carat cost}$$

The price/weight categories of colored gems vary from one dealer to another, so there's no point in listing any. Just be aware that carat weight can affect the per-carat value of gemstones and follow these two guidelines:

♦ Compare the per-carat prices of transparent gems instead of their total cost.

♦ When judging prices, compare stones of the same size, shape, quality and color.

Size Versus Carat Weight

Sometimes in the jewelry trade, the term "size" is used as a synonym for "carat weight." This is because size and weight are directly related. However, as gems increase in weight, their size becomes less predictable. This means a 0.90-ct emerald, for example, may look bigger than a 1.05-ct emerald. Therefore, you need to consider stone measurements as well as carat weight when buying colored stones. You don't need to carry a millimeter gauge with you when you go shopping. Just start noting the different illusions of size that various stone shapes and measurements can create.

You should also be aware that gemstones have varying densities. Consequently, stones of low density will look larger those of higher density. For example, because of its lower density, a one-carat emerald is considerably larger than a one-carat ruby. We can compare gem sizes by comparing their **specific gravity** (the ratio of a gem's density to the density of water).

Estimating Carat Weight

If you buy jewelry in a reputable jewelry store, you normally don't need to know how to estimate the carat weight of gems because the weight will be marked. However, if you buy jewelry at flea markets or garage sales, it is to your advantage to know how to estimate weight.

Appraisers estimate the weight of faceted gems by measuring their length, width and depth with a millimeter gauge (these are sold at jewelry supply stores). Then they calculate the weight with formulas such as the ones found in Table 3.2. The only accurate means of determining the weight of a stone is to take it out of its setting and weigh it. This, however, is not always possible or advisable.

Table 3.2 Weight Estimation Formulas for Faceted Gems	
Round	Diameter^2 x depth x S.G. x .0020
Oval	Diameter^2 x depth x S.G. x .0021 (Average out length and width to get diameter)
Rectangular Cushion	Diameter^2 x depth x S.G. x .00235 (Average length and width to get diameter)
Square Emerald Cut	Length x width x depth x S.G. x .0023
Rectangular Emerald Cut	Length x width x depth x S.G. x .0027
Square (with corners)	Length x width x depth x S.G. x .0025
Rectangular Baguette	Length x width x depth x S.G. x .0029
Pear	Length x width x depth x S.G. x .0020
Marquise	Length x width x depth x S. G. x .0021
Heart	Length x width x depth x S.G. x .00195

Note: S.G. = Specific Gravity. The specific gravity of the major gems is given in Chapter 11, "Gemstone Descriptions." The above formulas are based on stones with medium girdles, no pavilion bulge, and well-proportioned shapes. Thick girdles may require a correction of up to 10%. Bulging pavilions may require a correction as high as 18%. The correction for a poor shape outline can be up to 10%. For further information on weight estimation, consult the *Complete Handbook of Weight Estimation* by Charles Carmona.

4

Judging Color

Depending on whom you talk to, sherry-colored topaz is either yellow, orange, yellowish brown or reddish. That's because people have different opinions as to what is the color of sherry. Color terms like "sherry," "champagne" and "cognac" are great for displays and advertisements, but they are not appropriate for lab reports, appraisals and serious gemological texts since they don't give you a good visual idea of gem color.

Expressions like "grass green" are not much better. This term has been used in gemological literature to describe the color of peridot, alexandrite viewed outdoors, and fine emerald. That's understandable because grass comes in a wide range of greens. Most grasses, however, tend to be grayish or brownish, so it would be difficult to find grass with a top-grade emerald color.

For a more precise and accurate description of gems, it's helpful to divide color into the three components below. There are other ways to break down color; but this book uses the system employed by the Gemological Institute of America (GIA) and the American Gemological Laboratories (AGL).

Hue Refers to the basic colors of blue, green, yellow, orange, red, purple and violet as well as transition colors like bluish green and yellowish green. (Sometimes people are not sure of the difference between purple and violet. Violet falls between blue and purple. Purple is between red and violet so it is redder than violet.)

Lightness/darkness (Tone) Refers to the depth of color. The lightest possible tone is colorless. The darkest is black. **Tone** is another word for the degree of lightness or darkness. We'll describe tone in this book by the following terms:

very light   medium dark
light   dark
medium light   very dark
medium

Color purity The degree to which the hue is hidden by brown or gray. This book will describe color purity loosely with terms such as "highly pure" and "slightly brownish or grayish." Color purity is termed **saturation** in the GIA color grading system, and colors with a minimum amount of brown or gray are described as **vivid** or **strong**. The American Gemological Laboratories uses **intensity** to refer to color purity.

The terms **saturation** and **intensity** have other meanings as well. When some dealers describe the color of a stone as saturated, they mean it has both a high purity and good depth of color (tone). To them, a light pure color is neither saturated, nor strong, nor intense. "Saturation" sometimes only refers to the tone of pure colors. This is how it is used in GemDialogue, a color reference system used by many appraisers and jewelers.

A term such as "intense medium green" is less ambiguous than expressions like "grass green" and "sherry-colored." However, it's not as precise as using a color master stone or color sample as a reference point for describing gem color. Not everyone has the same visual image of intense medium green. So keep in mind that the color descriptions in this book are general, not precise. Nevertheless, they're better than "grass green," "cornflower blue" and "pigeon-blood red," terms which have often been used to describe the top color of emerald, sapphire and ruby.

Evaluating Gemstone Color

Even though it's debatable as to which are the most valuable hues and tones, gem dealers agree that pure, vivid colors are far more desirable than dull, muddy ones. In most high-quality stones, the bright areas of color should not look grayish or brownish.

Judging the **lightness or darkness** of a faceted gemstone is difficult because it doesn't display a single, uniform tone. It can have light and dark areas which become more apparent as you rock the stone in your hand. To judge the tone of a faceted gem, examine it face-up and answer the following questions:

♦ What is your first overall impression of the tone? How does it compare to that of other stones of the same variety? Use words such as "light" and "medium light" to describe tone, but keep in mind that the tonal boundaries of these terms can vary from one person and grading system to another. In most cases, medium to medium-dark tones are more valued than light and very dark tones.

The depth of color can play a major role in the price of gems. For example, a pure deep-green emerald selling for $5000 might be worth less than $100 if it were very light green. There's nothing inherently wrong, though, with light-green emeralds. In fact, they can be quite flattering to people who look good in pastel colors. It's just that there is a much greater demand for deep-green emeralds and their supply is more limited.

♦ Do you see near colorless, washed-out areas in the stone? This is a symbol of insufficient color, poor cutting or both.

♦ What percentage of the stone looks black? If more than 90% of a stone is blackish, gem dealers would classify it as undesirable, assuming that the stone is not black onyx or some other normally black stone. Many low-priced sapphires look black. Good sapphires are blue.

The GIA refers to the dark black or gray areas seen through the crown of faceted gems as **extinction**.. The amount of extinction you see depends on the tone, the cut, the type of lighting and the distance of the light from the stone. Light-colored, shallow-cut stones normally show less extinction than those which are dark-toned or deep-cut. As the light source gets broader, more diffused, and/or closer to stones, they display less extinction and more color.

Judging the **hue** of a stone is just as hard as judging the tone. The different tones within it are distracting. Moreover, it may be a blend of two or three colors. When you look at the stone from different directions while moving it, you can see the different colors. This is due to certain optical properties of the stone, which are discussed in Chapter 11, Gemstone Descriptions. This chapter also indicates the most valued hues for many of the important gem varieties. To determine the hue, look for the dominant color in the face-up view. Go with your first overall impression. Keep in mind that the most expensive hues are not necessarily the ones which will look best on you. If you don't plan to resell your stone, there's no need to base your choice of hue on trade preferences. Just choose the color you like best and that fits your budget.

Fig. 4.1 Color grading faceted gems is complicated because they frequently display a variety of colors simultaneously. When determining color, look for the average color reflected in the bright facet areas inside the stone. The 50-carat red-orange sapphire in this photo is a close match to AGL's Color/Scan reference number 242. *Photo courtesy AGL.*

How to Examine Color

When selecting a gemstone, follow these steps:

◆ Clean the stone with a soft cloth if it's dirty. Dirt and fingerprints hide color and brilliance.

◆ Examine the stone face up against a variety of backgrounds. Look straight down at it over a non-reflective, white background and check if the center of the stone is pale and washed out. (This is undesirable). Then look at it against a dark background. Do you still see glints of color or does most of the color disappear? Also, check how good the stone looks next to your skin.

◆ Examine the stone under direct light and away from it. Your stone won't always be spotlighted as you wear it. Does it still look colorful out of direct light? It should if it's of good quality.

◆ Look at the stone under various types of light available in the store. For example, check the color under an incandescent light-bulb, fluorescent light, and next to a window. If you're trying to match stones, it's particularly important to view them together under different lights. Stones that match under one light source may be mismatched under another.

Fig. 4.2 Burmese ruby with excellent color. *Ring and photo courtesy Color Masters Gem Corp.*

Fig. 4.3 Sapphire with excellent color. *Jewelry and photo courtesy Harry Winston, Inc.*

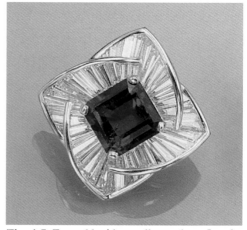

Fig. 4.4 Tanzanite with excellent color from Carrie G. Fine Gemstones

Fig. 4.5 Emerald with excellent color. *Jewelry and photo courtesy Harry Winston, Inc.*

◆ Every now and then, look away from the stone(s) and glance at other colors and objects to give your eyes a rest. When you focus too long on one color, your perception of it is distorted.

◆ Examine the stone for **color zoning**—the uneven distribution of color. When the color is uneven or concentrated in one spot, this can sometimes decrease the stone's value. It can also present a problem if the stone is recut. The color may become lighter. Obvious color zoning is most serious when visible in the face-up view of a stone.

◆ Compare the stone side-by-side with other stones of the same variety. Color nuances will be more apparent.

♦ Make sure you're alert and feel good when you examine stones. If you're tired, sick, or under the influence of alcohol or drugs, your perception of color will be impaired.

How Lighting Affects Gemstone Color

Visualize how different the colors of a snow-capped mountain are at sunrise and midday. This difference is due to the lighting, not to a change in the mountain itself. Likewise, the color of a gemstone will change depending on the lighting.

The whitest, most neutral light is at midday. Besides adding the least amount of color, this light makes it easier to see the various nuances of color. Consequently, you should judge gemstone color under a daylight-equivalent light. Neutral fluorescent bulbs approximate this ideal, but some of these lights are better than others. Three that are recommended are the Duro-Test Vita light, GE Chroma 50 or Sylvania Design 50. Even though gemstones are graded under daylight-equivalent light, many stones such as rubies and emeralds are often displayed and look their best under incandescent light (light bulbs).

When you shop for gems, your choice of lighting will probably be limited. Use the information below to help you compensate for improper lighting when you judge color. Some of the data is from "The Effects of Lighting on Gemstone Colors" by Howard Rubin.

Type of Lighting	Effect of Lighting on Gem Color
Sunlight	At midday, it normally has a neutral effect on the hue. Earlier and later in the day, it adds red, orange or yellow, making stones look more red, orange or purple.
Incandescent light bulbs, penlights and candlelight	Add red. Red colors are strengthened, warm colors appear more alike, grayish colors may look brownish, and green may look darker and a little more yellowish or less bluish.
Fluorescent lights	Depends on what type they are. Most strengthen blue colors. Warm white tubes add yellow.
Halogen spotlights	Add sparkle and usually add yellow.
Light under an overcast sky or in the shade	Adds blue and gray. Reds appear more purplish, greens and purples look more bluish, yellows look greener, and blues appear stronger.

Some stones such as alexandrite, tanzanite and color-change garnet and sapphire can change color under different lights. These stones should also be evaluated under an incandescent lamp (a pen-light is not a large enough light source). If a written appraisal is being done on the stone, the color under both fluorescent and incandescent light should be noted. Your final judgment of a gemstone, however, should be based on its appearance in daylight equivalent light.

Grading Color in Diamonds Versus Colored Stones

Grading color in colored stones would be much easier if a scale of 23 letter grades could adequately describe their color differences. Diamond color is graded with a scale like this extending from D to Z for **non-fancy colors** (colorless to light yellow, brown or gray). The jewelry trade, however, has not yet adopted a standardized system for grading colored stones. The following comparisons of the color grades and characteristics of diamonds and colored gems will help you understand why.

◆ Non-fancy diamond color grades only need to indicate the amount of color present (the tone). Colored-stone grades must also describe the hue and color purity to adequately explain price differences.

◆ Non-fancy diamond color grades represent a smaller range of tones than is needed for colored gems. The highest priced diamond tone, D, is colorless. Their lowest priced tone, Z, is a light tone. The tonal range of colored stones extends from very light to very dark. (Diamonds darker than Z are classified as fancy color, and their price usually escalates as the color become more saturated. There is no standardized color grading system for fancy-color diamonds.)

◆ Non-fancy diamond color grades are based mainly on the side view of the stone against a pure white background. Colored-stone grades are based mainly on the face-up view, which due to its many reflections is much harder to judge.

◆ Diamonds nearly always have one hue, if they are not colorless. Colored gems can exhibit two or three hues simultaneously, which complicates color grading. The cutting makes a difference in how the different hues combine in the face-up position. In certain directions, only one of the two or three colors is visible. The technical terms for this multi-color effect are **dichroism** and **trichroism**.

◆ Diamonds can be color-graded against master diamonds. The color comparison of colored stones is most often done using plastic, synthetic, and/or foil materials. These substances display color and reflect light differently than colored stones, so it's harder to describe these stones.

Some colored-gem dealers use stones from their own inventory for color comparison. They feel accurate gem grading is best achieved by referring to other stones of the same type. Assembling uniform sets of master colored gems, however, would be extremely expensive and time-consuming considering all their variations of hue, tone and color purity. As a result, no one has developed colored-stone master sets for general use.

◆ The lack of color is what's important in diamonds (unless they're fancy-colored diamonds). The quality of the color is what's important in colored stones; and for simplicity's sake, the descriptive terms used should be applicable to all colored gems for color comparison purposes. Naturally, a grading system that includes all colored stones will be far more complex than one just designed for diamonds.

Three Common Beliefs Which Warrant Review

♦ **Color is the most important factor for valuing colored stones.** Color is a major value factor, but it's not always the most important one. Suppose you have a fine $10,000-per-carat emerald. If it were translucent with the exact same color, it would be worth several times less, and transparency would be the main factor contributing to its lower value. Fractures in tanzanite can have a significant effect both on its price and salability. On the other hand, light purple colors can be very desirable even though they're priced lower than deep blues. If you examined the reject stones of colored stone dealers, you'd find that most of the stones were rejected because of poor clarity and/or transparency. This doesn't mean clarity is more important than color. It just indicates that the importance of each grading factor varies from one stone to another. Consumers who focus on color and play down other value factors risk getting a poor buy. When buying colored gems, remember—color is not everything, even though it does play a substantial role.

♦ **Color is just a matter of individual preference.** This is a common answer to the question, "What is the most valuable color?" The erroneous implication is that there are no trade standards for preferred colors. The pricing of colored gems is based on some universal principles regarding gem color—normally the less brown or gray present and the more saturated the color, the more valuable the stone. For each stone, there is also a range of hues which command a higher price than others. Even though your choice of color should be determined by what you like, you need to know how color is valued in order to accurately compare prices.

♦ **Dealers evaluate their stones in a logical, analytical manner.** Dealers tend to evaluate gem quality as a whole rather than breaking it down to its constituent parts of clarity, transparency, proportions, etc. Their final judgments are usually more intuitive than logical. In addition, non-quality-related factors also enter into their pricing of gems. Some of these price determinants are demand, form of payment, buyer's credit rating, amount purchased, and competitors' prices. Occasionally, you can find the same dealer selling a stone of higher quality for less than one of lower quality. This is because the rough for the higher quality stone may have cost less. Or, the rate of currency exchange could have been more favorable at the time of purchase. Therefore, you should not assume that higher price necessarily means higher quality. Conversely, lower price is not necessarily indicative of a deal.

Since you can't always count on prices to reflect the quality of gems, it's all the more important that you learn to make quality judgments yourself. The reason this book analyzes color and gem quality in terms of their component parts is to aid you in this process. Vague statements such as "look for color" or "grass green is best" are not very helpful to consumers. However, when you learn how the color elements of hue, tone and color purity affect the price of a gem, it's easier for you to understand gem valuation. Your ultimate goal should be to reach the level where you can make quick global judgments about gem quality. But like any other skill, this takes practice.

5

Judging Clarity & Transparency

Clarity and transparency are very important value factors for gems, sometimes even more important than color. Consider, for example, emeralds or sapphires. No matter how grayish, brownish, and/or light-colored they are, they're still gems if they are transparent and **eye-clean** (free of flaws visible to the unaided eye). The term **clean** by itself can mean that a stone is of high clarity. However, if they are opaque and filled with deep cracks and eye-visible flaws, they're industrial grade stones, even if they have a desirable color.

Some gems are more likely to have flaws than others. Emeralds, for example, typically have some eye-visible flaws. Aquamarine, on the other hand, is normally eye clean. As a result, there is a greater tolerance for noticeable flaws in emerald than in aquamarine. Three other gems that usually have eye-visible flaws are ruby, alexandrite and red tourmaline. Some of the stones that typically have a high clarity like aquamarine are blue zircon, citrine, green tourmaline, green and yellow chrysoberyl, kunzite, topaz and tanzanite. Some colored gems that fall between these high- and low-clarity groups include amethyst, blue tourmaline, garnet, iolite, peridot, spinel and zircon that is green, orange or red. The chart on the next page gives a more visual representation of the typical clarity range of some of the most important colored gems.

Fig. 5.1 This 2-carat Russian alexandrite wholesaled for $13,000 in 1997 although it has several crystal inclusions. (Approximate color under incandescent light)

Fig. 5.2 Approximate size

Fig. 5.3 Same stone as it appears in daylight. A color change as distinct as this is rare in alexandrite. The flaws are typical.

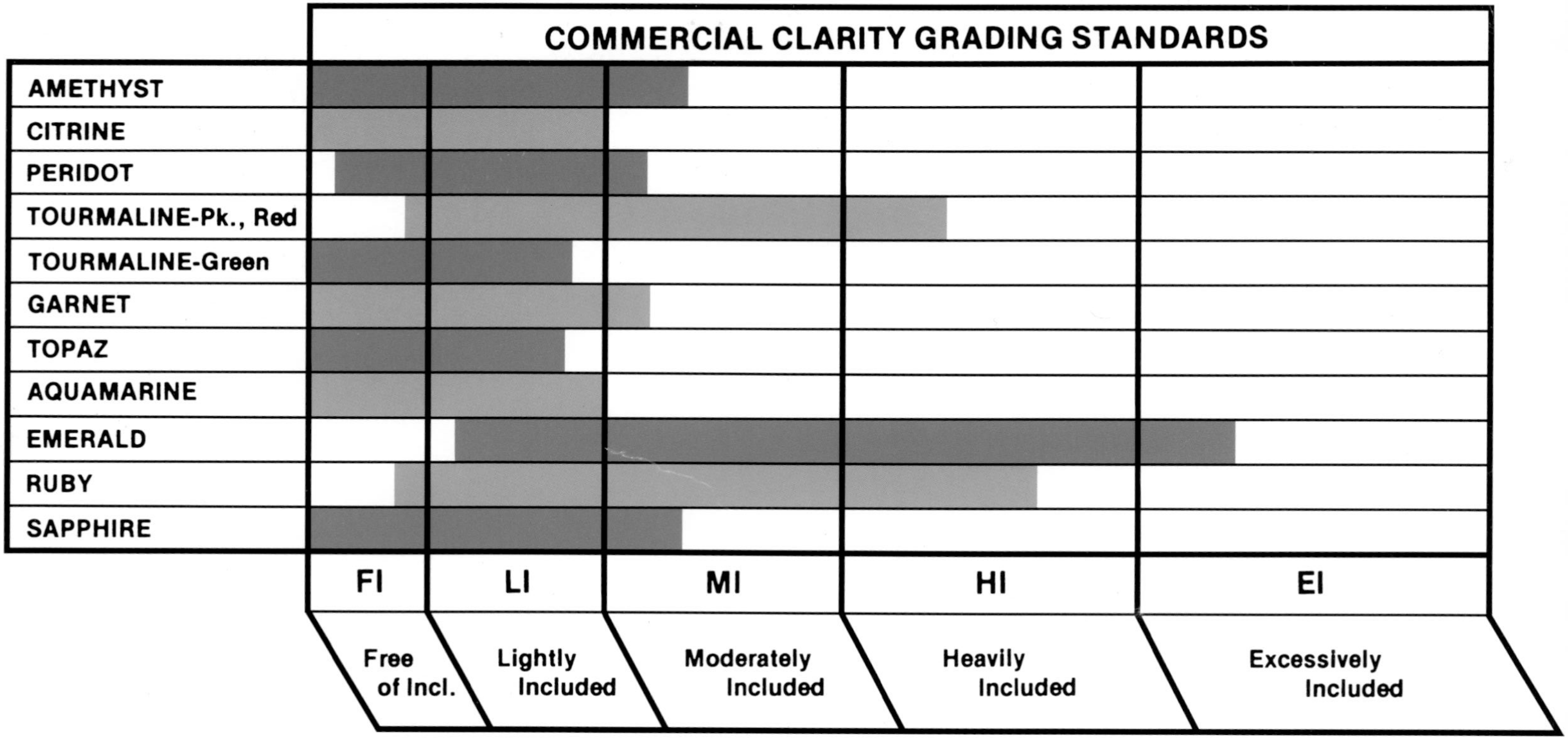

COMMERCIAL CLARITY GRADING STANDARDS

	FI	LI	MI	HI	EI
	Free of Incl.	Lightly Included	Moderately Included	Heavily Included	Excessively Included

AMETHYST

CITRINE

PERIDOT

TOURMALINE-Pk., Red

TOURMALINE-Green

GARNET

TOPAZ

AQUAMARINE

EMERALD

RUBY

SAPPHIRE

Table 5.1 This clarity chart shows the relationship between various colored stones and indicates the limits of clarity that are generally acceptable to most jewelry manufacturers and stone dealers. A heavily flawed ruby, for example, is more salable than a sapphire of the same clarity. Emeralds generally have more flaws than other gemstones. The lines represent where the bulk of the commercial material lies for each gem. *Diagram copyright 1976 by AGL (American Gemological Laboratories).*

Before continuing this chapter, let's explain some basic terminology. **Clarity** is the degree to which a stone is free from flaws. Gemologists call flaws within a stone **inclusions**. Flaws on a stone's surface are **blemishes**. A general term for inclusions and blemishes is **clarity characteristics.** In this book, "flaw" is often used because it is shorter and clearer. Some trade members believe the use of the word "flaw" creates customer resistance to gems. When inclusions and blemishes are properly explained, it doesn't matter what they are called. Customers will learn to accept them as a normal characteristic of natural gemstones. Flaws do generally have a negative impact on value, but this is good news for the buyer. They can make a gem more affordable, without necessarily affecting its beauty.

Transparency is the degree to which light passes through a material so that objects are visible through it. Transparency and clarity are interlinked because flaws can block the passage of light. Gemologists use the following terms to describe gem transparency.

♦ **Transparent**—objects seen through the stone look clear and distinct.

♦ **Semitransparent**—objects look slightly hazy or blurry through the stone.

♦ **Translucent**—objects are vague and hard to see. Imagining what it is like to read print through frosted glass will help you understand the concept of translucency.

♦ **Semitranslucent** or **semi-opaque**—a small fraction of light passes through the stone, mainly around the edges.

♦ **Opaque**—virtually no light passes through the stone. When classifying the transparency of a gem variety, "opaque" is considered to refer to specimens of ordinary thickness, because in thin slices most "opaque" substances transmit some light.

Occasionally, **near transparent** is used as a category between transparent and semitransparent, The most transparent specimens of jade and opal can fit in this category as well as many high-quality emeralds and rubies.

Another word that refers to transparency is **texture.** AGL (American Gemological Laboratories) in New York applies this term to fine particles which interrupt the passage of light in a material. The finely divided particles are not detrimental to the durability of a stone, but they can have an adverse effect on its appearance. Yet texture is not always a negative factor. The texture within Kashmir sapphire, for example, gives it a prized velvety appearance. AGL, on its lab documents, describes the texture (transparency) of colored stones as follows:

♦ Faint texture: very slightly hazy
♦ Moderate texture: cloudy
♦ Strong texture: translucent
♦ Prominent texture: semitranslucent or opaque

Texture can also refer to the fineness of the tiny crystal components of rock-like gem materials. For example, jade can have a fine to coarse texture depending on the size of its interlocking crystal constituents, which are ideally microscopic.

Dealers often use other terms to designate gem transparency, some of which are:

♦ crystal (highly transparent)   ♦ cloudy
♦ highly transparent   ♦ looks like soap
♦ milky   ♦ sleepy (has low transparency)

Jade dealers often use **translucency** instead of the term "transparency." Dealers of opal, another opaque to near transparent gem, generally prefer to use "transparency." For the sake of consistency, this book uses "transparency" for all gems when referring to how easily light can pass through them. It's easier to understand gemstone evaluation when the same terminology is used for every gemstone. Whether a gem is traditionally considered as transparent or translucent, transparency can play a major role in its value. Don't overlook this when comparing the prices of gemstones.

Examining Gemstones for Clarity

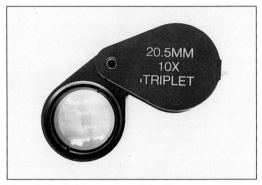

Fig. 5.4 A 10-power triplet loupe

To examine a stone for clarity you need a ten-power magnifier, a lint free cloth and a light source with a translucent shade or with a bulb that's frosted—not bare. An ordinary fluorescent desk lamp will do. Tweezers or a stone-holder is also helpful. Jewelers often use a hand magnifier called a loupe. For those interested in owning a loupe, the business section of the phone book has stores listed under *Jewelers' Supplies & Findings*. First verify that they have a fully corrected, ten-power, triplet loupe. The loupe salesman or a jeweler can show you some ways of holding and using it and help you select the model that is the most comfortable and clear. Plan on paying at least $25 for a good loupe. Cheaper types, which are not fully corrected, tend to distort objects.

When using a ten-power loupe, hold it about 1/2 to 1 inch (13-25 mm.) away from the stone to bring it into focus. If you're examining a large stone, hold the loupe close to one eye (about 1 or 2 inches or 25-50 mm. from the eye) keeping both eyes open. The closer the loupe is to your eye, the greater your field of vision will be.

Often it's easier for lay people to examine stones through a microscope. Many jewelers own microscopes and encourage their customers to use it when purchasing gemstones.

When you have the necessary equipment, you can proceed as follows:

♦ **Clean the stone.** Otherwise, you may think dirt and spots are inclusions. Usually rubbing it with a lint-free cloth is sufficient. If you're examining jewelry at home, it may have to be cleaned with water. (See Chapter 11 for cleaning instructions.) Professional cleaning might also be necessary. Avoid touching the stone with your fingers as fingers can leave smudges.

♦ **Examine the entire stone without magnification.** (However, if you require eyeglasses for reading, you'll need to wear them when examining gems.) One of the main criteria for assessing the clarity of colored gems is the visibility of the inclusions with the naked eye. Looking at the stone first with a loupe or microscope can mislead you into believing inclusions are eye visible when they aren't, because your mind has a tendency to see what it expects to see. So check to see if there are any noticeable flaws before using magnification. If you are

46

looking at a good topaz, aquamarine or tanzanite, you shouldn't see any. A good ruby or emerald, on the other hand, is likely to have eye-visible inclusions. However, the fewer flaws it has, the higher its value.

Check, too, the overall transparency of the stone. If your goal is to buy a high-quality transparent gemstone, avoid cloudy or opaque stones.

♦ **Look at the stone from several angles**—top, bottom, sides. Even though top and centrally-located inclusions are the most undesirable in terms of beauty, those seen from the sides or bottom of a stone can affect its price or durability.

♦ **Look at the stone also with light shining through it from the side** (transmitted light). This will help you see flaws inside the stone. It will also help you judge transparency.

♦ **Look at the stone with light shining on it from various angles**—above it, through the sides, and reflected off the surfaces. Overhead illumination will help you determine what the blemishes and inclusions look like under normal lighting conditions. Light transmitted through the sides will highlight inclusions and will usually make them more visible. Light reflected off the surface will help you identify surface cracks and blemishes.

♦ **When you judge clarity, compare stones of the same type.** Emeralds, for example, should be compared to emeralds, not to other gems, which typically have a higher clarity. Tanzanite, a very transparent, clean stone, should be compared to other tanzanites, not to sapphire, which tends to be more included.

♦ **Keep in mind that light-colored stones should have a better clarity than darker ones.** In lighter stones, inclusions are easier to see. Dark colors often mask flaws.

♦ **Remember that prongs and settings can hide flaws.** If you're interested in a stone with a high clarity, it may be best for you to buy a loose stone and have it set.

♦ **Keep in mind that your overall impression of a stone's clarity can be affected by the stones it is compared to.** A stone will look better when viewed next to one of low clarity than next to one of high clarity. To have a more balanced outlook, try to look at a variety of qualities.

How Lighting Can Affect Your Perception of Clarity

You should judge the clarity of colored stones using overhead lighting both with and without magnification. A loupe (hand magnifier) or a microscope can help you see potentially damaging flaws that might escape the unaided eye.

When people use microscopes to judge clarity, they usually examine the stones with a type of lighting called **darkfield illumination**. This is a diffused lighting that comes up diagonally through the bottom of the stone. (A frosted or shaded bulb provides **diffused** light, a clear bulb does not.) In this lighting, tiny inclusions and even dust particles will stand out in high relief. As a result, the clarity of the stone appears worse than it would under normal conditions (figures 5.2 and 5.3 provide examples of this).

Overhead lighting is above the stone (not literally over a person's head). It is reflected off the facets whereas darkfield lighting is transmitted through the stone. When looking at jewelry

 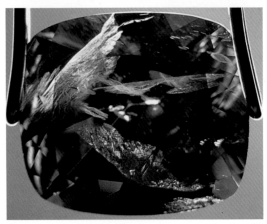

Fig. 5.5 An iolite in overhead light. From the standpoint of appearance, the clarity is not bad. However, large cracks in the stone threaten its durability.

Fig. 5.6 Darkfield illumination turns the hardly noticeable cracks into distracting inclusions. Ten-power magnification through a microscope was used for this stone in both photos.

with the unaided eye, you normally view it in overhead lighting. However, if you ask salespeople to show you a stone under a microscope, it is unlikely that they will use its overhead lamp. Instead they may only have you view the stone under darkfield illumination.

When judging colored-stone clarity under magnification, you should use overhead lighting for the following reasons:

♦ **Dealers use overhead lighting when pricing gems**. They typically examine stones under a fluorescent lamp with and without a loupe (usually 10-power).

♦ **Overhead illumination is a natural way of lighting which does not exaggerate flaws.** It therefore helps you make a fair assessment of a stone's appearance.

♦ **Overhead lighting does not hide brilliance**. The prime reason for looking at gems through loupes and microscopes is to see their beauty and brilliance magnified. Darkfield illumination masks brilliance. Consequently, it prevents you from making an accurate global assessment of a gem under magnification.

After using overhead lighting, you should also view stones under darkfield illumination. It highlights inclusion details which are useful for detecting synthetics, treatments, and place of origin. With emeralds, for example, darkfield illumination can help you determine the depth of cracks, the type of filling present in fractures, and the extent to which an emerald may have been treated to hide cracks. In summary, darkfield lighting is a useful diagnostic aid, but it can be misleading when used for judging the clarity of colored stones.

Gemstone Inclusions

Opinions differ as to how various clarity features should be classified. Some feel the term "inclusion" should be reserved for foreign matter within a stone. This book uses a broader definition, which is found in the GIA gemstone courses: "**Inclusions** are characteristics which are

48

Figs. 5.7 & 5.8 Two views of an emerald with liquid inclusions and fractures—one in darkfield illumination under 10-power magnification and another in overhead lighting with less magnification.

entirely inside a stone or that extend into it from the surface." The GIA defines **blemishes** as "characteristics confined to or primarily affecting the surface."

As you examine stones under magnification, you'll probably wonder what inclusions you are looking at. Listed below are gemstone inclusions found in colored stones:

◆ **Crystals** are solid mineral inclusions of various shapes and sizes. Minute crystals that look like small specks under 10X magnification are sometimes called **pinpoints** or **grains**. Crystals lower the clarity, but they can also turn a stone into a collector's item if they are unusual and attractive. The larger and more visible the crystals are, the more they impact the clarity.

◆ **Negative crystals or voids** are hollow spaces inside a stone that have the shape of a crystal. They often resemble solid crystals, so for purposes of clarity grading, they're just called "included crystals."

◆ **Clouds** are hazy or milky areas in a stone. Most clouds are made up of crystals too tiny to see individually under ten-power magnification. When clouds are large and dense, they diminish transparency.

◆ **Needles** are long, thin inclusions that are either solid crystals or tubes filled with gas or liquid, which are called **growth tubes**.

◆ **Silk** in gemstones consists of very fine fibers of minerals such as rutile (titanium dioxide). It can also be made of mineral grains arranged in straight rows. These fibers or rows intersect and resemble silk, hence the name. Well-formed silk can be proof that a stone was not heat-treated to improve its color. Very high temperatures tend to dissolve it and make it look fuzzy or dot-like. Since untreated stones tend to be more valued than treated ones, the presence of clear, well-formed silk can be a welcome sign.

◆ **Cracks** of various sizes are not uncommon. They may also be called **fractures** or **breaks**. When they're straight and flat, they're called **cleavages**. Because of their appearance, cracks are sometimes called **feathers**. Normally, you need not worry about cracks if they are small. However, if they are deep or long, they can threaten the durability of the stone. The location of the cracks is also important. Surface cracks on the table of a stone have a very negative impact on value. A crack in the center of the stone is much easier to see with the naked eye than one close to the edge.

◆ **Halos** are circular fractures surrounding a crystal. These structures generally result from tension created by the growth of the crystal inside the halo or by heat treatment.

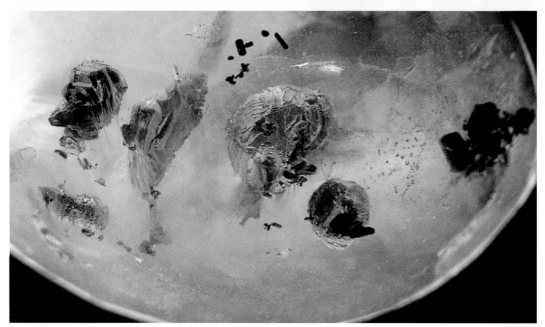

Fig. 5.9 Crystal inclusions in a light blue sapphire cabochon

♦ **Liquid inclusions** are hollow spaces filled with fluid. They occur in random shapes and sometimes are so dense that the stone may look milky. The GIA classifies liquid inclusions into three types: **single-phase**, a void containing only liquid; **two-phase**, a liquid and a gas or two nonmixable liquids; and **three-phase**, a liquid, a gas and a solid.

♦ **Fingerprints** are partially healed cracks. Many colored gems grow from a mineral solution, and if they split during formation, the solution can fill the cracks and let them grow back together. During this healing process, stray drops of liquid are sealed in and form patterns that look like human fingerprints.

♦ **Growth or color zoning** refers to an uneven distribution of color in a stone. If the different color zones look like bands, they are called **growth or color bands**. This is usually visible under 10X magnification. If visible to the unaided eye, color zoning may be undesirable

♦ **Cavities** are holes or indentations extending into a stone from the surface. Cavities can result when solid crystals are pulled out of a stone or when negative crystals are exposed during the cutting process.

♦ **Chips** are notches or broken off pieces of stone often along the girdle edge or at the culet.

Gemstone Blemishes

♦ **Scratches** are straight or crooked lines scraped on a stone. Since they can be polished away, they don't have much of an effect on the clarity.

♦ **Pits** are tiny holes on the surface of a stone that often look like white dots.

♦ **Abrasions** are rough, scraped areas usually along the facet edges of a stone. They are seen

Do We Need Grades to Evaluate Clarity and Transparency?

The diamond industry has a standardized system for grading clarity based on a system developed by the GIA. Ten-power magnification is used. The advantage of having this system is that buyers can communicate what they want anywhere in the world. In addition, written appraisals and quality reports are more meaningful.

One of the drawbacks of the diamond grading system is that it has sometimes caused buyers to become so focused on color and clarity that they overlook brilliance and cut. Another drawback is that it has led people to judge stones by grades rather than with their eyes. No grade or lab report can give a full picture of what a stone looks like. In addition, grades are often misrepresented. Without examining a stone under magnification, one cannot tell if a grade has been inflated.

Even though clarity grading systems have been developed for colored stones, there is no one standardized system. Even when a single system is used, there can be a wide variation in how grades are assigned by appraisers, mainly because the way in which transparency is incorporated into the system may differ. Therefore, it's best for you to ask your appraiser what his or her grades mean. Grades are helpful for documentation purposes, but you don't need them to judge clarity and transparency.

6

Judging Cut

C ut plays a major role in determining the value of colored gems because it affects their color and clarity as well as their brilliance. For example, a stone that is cut too shallow can look pale and lifeless, and it can display flaws that would normally not be visible to the naked eye.

The term **cut** is sometimes confusing because it has a variety of meanings. Jewelers use it to refer to:

♦ The **shape** of a gemstone (e.g. round or oval)

♦ The **cutting style** (e.g. cabochon or faceted, brilliant or step cut, single or full cut)

♦ The **proportions** of a stone (e.g. pavilion depth, girdle thickness)

♦ The **finish** of a stone (e.g. polishing marks or smooth flawless surface, misshapen or symmetrical facets)

The proportions and finish are also called the **make** of the stone. Proportions and how they affect the appearance of emeralds and tanzanites will be the focus of this chapter. Shape and cutting style were discussed in Chapter 2. Finish will not be discussed because it normally does not have much of an effect on the price of colored stones. If there is a problem with the finish, it can usually be corrected by repolishing the stone. Blemishes such as scratches and abrasions are sometimes considered as part of the finish grade of the stone. This book classifies them as clarity elements.

Judging the Face-up View

Colored stones should display maximum color. However, if they're cut with improper angles, their color potential can be diminished with what is called a **window**—a washed out area in the middle of the stone that allows you to see right through it. Windows (or windowing) can occur in any transparent, faceted stone no matter how light or dark it is and no matter how deep or shallow its pavilion. In general, the larger the window, the poorer the cut. Windowed stones are the attempt of the cutter to maximize weight at the expense of brilliance.

To look for windows, hold the stone about an inch or two (2 to 5 cm) above a contrasting background such as your hand or a piece of white paper. Then try to look straight through the top of the stone **without tilting it**, and check if you can see the background or a light window-like area in the center of it. If the stone is light colored, you might try holding it above a printed page to see if the print shows through. If the center area of the stone is pale or lifeless compared to a darker faceted area surrounding the pale center, this is also a window effect.

Fig. 6.1 A kunzite with no window

Fig. 6.2 Face-up view of an amethyst with an extremely large window through which print is visible

Fig. 6.3 Ametrine with a distracting window

Fig. 6.4 Color-change garnets with moderate windows

When evaluating a stone for windowing, you will probably notice dark areas in it. The GIA refers to these as **extinction areas** or simply **extinction**. All transparent faceted gems have some dark areas. However, a good cut can reduce extinction and increase color. One should expect dark stones to have a higher percentage of dark areas than those which are lighter colored. You should also expect there to be more extinction than what you see in pictures of gems. During shooting, photographers normally use two or more front lights to make stones show as much color as possible. When you look at a stone, you will usually be using a single light source, so less color and more black will show. The broader and more diffused the light is, the more colorful the stone will look. Therefore, compare stones under the same type and amount of lighting.

The quality, complexity and originality of the faceting should also be considered when judging cut. Some of the best faceting is done on low- and medium-priced gem material such as aquamarine, garnet, quartz, tanzanite, topaz and tourmaline. The faceting and proportioning of more expensive stones like emeralds and rubies is often less precise because the higher cost of the rough leads many cutters to be more interested in retaining weight than in maximizing beauty. Finding an emerald or ruby without windowing can be difficult. Nevertheless, emeralds, rubies and other expensive stones can be well-cut and display good color and brilliance. For more photos and information on faceting styles, see Chapter 2.

When you hear the term **brilliance** used, keep in mind that it has different definitions. In the GIA Colored Stone Grading Course, it is defined as the percentage of light return in a gem after the percentage of windowing and extinction are subtracted. AGL (American Gemological Laboratories) uses "brilliance" only in connection with the amount of windowing present. A stone with no window whatsoever would receive a brilliance grade of 100%. This high of a brilliance percentage would not be possible under the GIA system because there is always some extinction present in transparent faceted gems. In this book, the term "brilliant" is used in the colloquial sense of having both a high intensity and large area of light return. A dull-looking, low-transparency stone with no window would not be described as "brilliant" under this non-technical definition.

Another thing to notice when judging the face-up view of a gem is the outline of the shape. If it's a standard shape that should be symmetrical, check to see if it is. If you plan to resell the stone later, make sure it's a shape others might like. A very long, skinny marquise or emerald cut, for example, may be hard to sell. With stones such as ruby, emerald and alexandrite, conserving weight from the rough is often more of a priority than good symmetry.

Judging the Profile

When you buy a gemstone, be sure to look at its profile. The side view can indicate:

♦ If the stone is suitable for mounting in jewelry.

♦ If the stone will look big or small for its weight.

♦ If the cutter's main goal was to bring out the stone's brilliance.

When evaluating the profile, hold the stone with the shortest side facing you (widthwise) and **check the overall depth** (referred to in the trade as the **total depth percentage**). If you look at it lengthwise, the stone could look too shallow when in fact it may have an adequate depth.

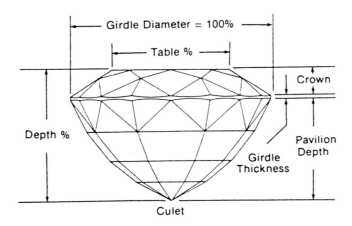

Fig. 6.5 Profile diagram of a mixed-cut colored stone. *Copyright 1978 by American Gemological Laboratories, Inc.*

Fig. 6.6 A yellow-orange sapphire with no window and a good play of light and color off the facets

Fig. 6.7 Side view of same stone. Sapphires with good brilliance are typically deeper than diamonds. This stone is a little deep for some mountings.

You should expect well-cut colored stones to be deeper than diamonds, which have a high refractive index (a measure of the degree to which light is bent as it travels through a gem).

Noted mineralogist John Sinkankas makes this point in his book, *Emerald and Other Beryls* (page 334): "In the case of higher refractive index gemstones, inner reflections can result from shallower bottom angles, thus allowing these gems to be cut less deeply. This becomes apparent when two brilliant gems of the same size and style of cutting are compared, one being diamond and the other a beryl. It will be seen that the diamond is cut to less depth while the beryl had to be cut to greater depth in order to insure upward reflection of light."

The **total depth percentage** of the stone in the profile diagram of figure 6.5 can be calculated as follows:

depth
width (girdle diameter)

In this case, the total depth percentage is 65%, which is a good depth/width ratio for a colored stone. There are differences of opinion as to which is the best depth percentage for a colored stone cut in a traditional style such as an emerald cut or round brilliant cut. Some say 60 to 65%. Others say 65 to 80%. Combining these two ranges, we can conclude that a stone's depth should range between 60 to 80% of its width.

If a stone is too deep, it may not be suitable for mounting in jewelry and it will look small for its weight in the face-up view. The main reason for cutting extremely deep stones is to save as much weight from the original rough as possible. Stones may also be cut deep to darken their color, especially if they are pale or color-zoned. Unnecessary weight adds to the cost of the stone since prices are calculated by multiplying the weight times the per-carat cost. Consequently, when you compare the prices of stones, you should consider their overall depth.

If a stone is extremely shallow ("flat") when you look at it widthwise, it might be fragile and therefore unsuitable as a stone for an everyday ring (it could, however, be good for a pendant, brooch or earrings). Very shallow stones look big for their weight in the face-up view, but unfortunately they often have big windows and lack life, which brings down their value. The main reason for cutting extremely shallow stones is to maintain the shape of the original rough so

Fig. 6.8 Profile of the amethyst in figure 6.2. The pavilion is so shallow that it creates a large window.

Fig. 6.9 A tanzanite with a thin crown

as not to lose too much weight. Stones may also be cut shallow to lighten their color. Some cutters are able to take flat gem rough and cut it into attractive, brilliant stones using non-traditional cutting styles. The Torus Ring™ is an example of this. It faces up larger than a normal stone of the same weight without any sacrifice to brilliance. In this case, the total depth percentage of the gemstone is irrelevant. What matters is the overall appearance.

When judging the profile of a gemstone, you should also pay attention to the **crown height and the pavilion depth.** Notice the relationship of the crown height to the pavilion depth in the profile diagram of figure 6.5 (about 3.5 to 1). Then compare the profile views in this chapter to the diagram. Without even measuring these stones, you can make visual judgments about their pavilion and crown heights.

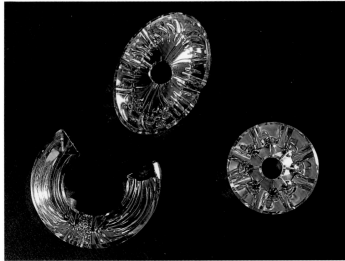

Fig. 6.10 This amethyst, concave faceted by Mark Gronlund, has excellent brilliance and no window. It's well cut, even though some of its proportions may not meet traditional standards.

Fig. 6.11 Ring-shaped ametrines and amethyst (Torus Rings™) carved and photographed by Glenn Lehrer. These are examples of how a skilled, imaginative cutter can bring out brilliance, yet minimize weight loss in flat rough.

If the **crown** is too low, the stone will lack sparkle. When light falls on a flat crown, there tends to be a large sheet-like reflection off the table facet instead of twinkles of light from the other crown facets. Some cutters intentionally cut stones with no crowns in order to draw your eye into the interior of the stone. This is commonly seen in fantasy-style cuts. These stones should be judged on their general appearance, not according to traditional standards.

If the **pavilion** is too flat or too deep, the stone may lack life, have a window, or look blackish. In order for the stone to effectively reflect light, the pavilion and crown must be angled properly. But they can't have the proper angles if they don't have the proper depth.

While evaluating the profile, look at the curvature of the pavilion outline. A lumpy, bulging pavilion decreases brilliance and helps create dark or window-like areas in the stone. This is because the pavilion is not slanted at an angle that will maximize light reflection. A bulging pavilion is not uncommon in expensive stones. It's another example of how you can end up paying for excess weight that reduces the beauty of the stone. Unlike diamonds, colored stones should have a slight pavilion curvature. This helps decrease windowing as the stone is tilted.

Notice, too, the **symmetry** of the profile. Symmetry problems such as an **off-center culet** prevent light from reflecting evenly. (In cushions, ovals and marquises, the culet should be centered widthwise and lengthwise. In hearts and pear-shapes, the culet should be placed at the widest portion of the stone.) It's common for rubies, emeralds, sapphires and alexandrites to look less symmetrical than stones such as diamonds. However, when stones are so lopsided that their brilliance is seriously diminished, the lack of symmetry is unacceptable.

Also check the **girdle width**. Stones with very thin girdles are difficult to set and easy to chip. Stones with thick girdles have reduced brilliance, look smaller than they weigh, and are also difficult to set. The judgment of girdle thickness is best done with the eye, with and without magnification. If the girdle looks like a wide band encircling the stone, it's probably too thick. If the girdle is sharp and you can hardly see it, then it's probably too thin. **Wavy and uneven girdles** can also create setting problems. In addition, they indicate that the cutter did not pay much attention to detail.

How Cut Affects Price

Theoretically, major cutting defects should reduce gem prices substantially. In actual practice, this is not always true.

Sometimes the cut may have no direct effect on the per-carat price. For example a 1/2-carat sapphire pendant may be mass-produced and sold at the same price in chain stores. Some of the sapphires may be well-cut. Others of similar color and clarity may have large windows. In spite of their identical price, the value of the better-cut sapphires should be greater.

In some stores, you can select a gem from an assortment of stones in a packet or little bowl. The per-carat price for all the stones may be the same even though they might vary considerably in quality. People who know how to judge cut, color, clarity, and transparency will get the best buys in cases like these because they will be able to pick out the most valuable stones and avoid paying for unnecessary weight.

Sometimes the cut has a mathematically calculated effect on the price of gems. For example, the prices of fine-quality princess cuts that are calibrated to specific millimeter size may be determined by the weight lost when cutting the stones.

If you were to have a large stone recut to bring out its brilliance, you could calculate its new per-carat price by dividing the new weight into the combined cost of the recutting and the stone.

The increased value of a stone after recutting can more than make up for its lost weight and cutting costs. Consequently, it is not uncommon for fine-quality gem material to be recut to improve the proportions. There are risks, however, to recutting gems. Their value may decrease due to breakage or color lightening.

Sometimes the cut affects prices in a subjective manner. Some dealers place a greater importance on cut than others, and they may discount a very poorly cut stone as much as 50% in order to sell it. Another dealer might discount the same stone 25%. Premiums of between 10 to 25% may be added to precision-cut stones. But considering the fact that fine-cut stones don't have unnecessary weight, their total cost may not be much more than that of a bulky stone with the same face-up size.

There is no established trade formula for determining percentage-wise how cut affects the value of gems. There is, however, agreement that a well-proportioned, brilliant stone is more valuable than one which is poorly cut. As you shop, you may discover that well-cut stones are not always readily available, particularly in the case of emeralds and rubies. This is unfortunate because man has control over a stone's cut. Cutting has improved over the last five years because of demands from customers. Achieving brilliance is becoming more important than saving weight. If this trend continues, it will be easier for you to find well-cut gems.

Judging "Life"

The term "life" is frequently used by dealers to refer to the overall brilliance and sparkle of a gem. Some people equate it to "cut," but it's different because a stone can be well-cut yet have poor life. Even though it is one of the most important value factors, "life" is not listed as a grading category on gem lab reports or appraisals—probably because it's difficult to define and quantify. It's subjective. Some of the factors that can influence your impression of "life" are:

Transparency. The higher the transparency the greater the life. This is a key factor in determining life in stones such as ruby and emerald, which due to inclusions, tend to have a lower transparency than most other "transparent gems".

Faceting style. Brilliant- and mixed-cut stones generally have more life than step cuts. Step-cut stones, such as emerald cuts, can look lively, but one's expectation of life in those stones should be lower. Stones with concave facets may display greater brilliance than those with flat facets.

Proportions. Well-proportioned stones will return more light to the eye than poorly cut stones with windows. A gem can be well proportioned, though, and still lack life.

Polish. The higher the polish, the brighter a gem will look. Hard stones can take a higher polish than softer stones, so there are different expectations of polish luster depending on the gem species.

Clarity. Inclusions can impede light and brilliance, thereby lowering the life of a gem.

Amount of gray present. Often the more grayish a stone is the duller it looks. This is one of the reasons grayish stones tend to be less valued than stones with purer colors. Even gray diamonds can look dull, which is probably why at the wholesale level, they may cost less than yellowish diamonds of the same tone.

Tone. The lighter a stone is the more brilliant it can be. Keep in mind, though, that deep, saturated colors are much more highly valued than light colors.

Sometimes we get so involved in analyzing the color, clarity and cut of gems that we forget to notice if they have "life." As you browse in jewelry stores, make a special effort to notice the overall brilliance of the gems. This helps develop the eye. Once you can recognize a fine-cut, lively stone, you'll be well on your way to spotting value.

7

Star & Cat's-Eye Stones

C abochons (gems with a domed, polished surface) can resemble a cat's eye when they have many needle-like inclusions or hollow tubes, all parallel to each other, and are cut properly. When the cabochon is placed under a concentrated light source such as a light bulb, a band of reflected light is visible across the top of the cabochon. This effect is called **chatoyancy**, and stones that display it are said to be **chatoyant**. *(Chat* means "cat" in French.)

The term "cat's-eye" when used by itself also refers to the chatoyant variety of chrysoberyl, a gem species. Other minerals such as beryl, quartz, tourmaline and zircon can also display a cat's-eye, but these stones must include the mineral name—for example, "cat's-eye quartz" or "quartz cat's-eye." Besides the cat's-eye effect, these stones may show what is called the **"milk and honey effect"** (fig. 7.2)—when the stone is held with the eye at a right angle to a beam of light, the half of the stone nearest the light shows the body color of the stone, while the other half looks milky. When the stone is rotated between two lights, the chatoyant band appears to open and close. The open position is shown in figure 7.3.

Top-quality cat's-eye stones have the following characteristics:

◆ They have a sharp, straight, narrow band (eye) positioned in the center of the cabochon. The band is distinct and not too thin.
◆ The band of reflected light is white or gray, not the same color hue as the stone's background.
◆ The eye extends all the way across the stone.
◆ The stone has no distracting flaws.
◆ The stone is neither opaque or transparent.

Unfortunately, there are not many stones that meet all these criteria. When buying gemstones it's often necessary to compromise on some quality factors. Don't expect cat's-eye stones to be free of eye-visible flaws or to have perfect symmetry. Don't worry if a little of the stones color shows through in the eye. The most important consideration when buying a chatoyant gem is that it has a distinct eye.

The needle inclusions in cat's-eye stones line up in one direction like thread on a spool; but in some gems they align them-

Fig. 7.1 Cat's-eye

61

Fig. 7.2 Milk and honey effect

Fig. 7.3 Opening and closing effect

selves in groups oriented in different directions. When these stones are cut as cabochons, the bands of reflected light may cross each other in the center, creating a star. This effect is called **asterism**. The half of a band that starts from the center of the stone and goes to the edge is called a **ray**. Star gems generally have from four to twelve rays. Star rubies and star sapphires are the best known star gems. Other gems that can display a star include beryl, garnet, quartz and spinel.

In 1947, synthetic star ruby and sapphire stones were introduced to the market by the Linde Division of the Union Carbide Corporation in the United States. They were an instant success, and ever since that time there has been a tendency to expect natural stones to resemble them. It's true that there are some very fine deep blue and red specimens in museums and private collections, but these are the exception rather than the rule. Most natural star sapphires are normally more pale than natural faceted sapphires, and their stars are not as well defined as those of laboratory-grown (synthetic) stones. Star rubies often have a maroon rather than red color and their stars tend to be indistinct and imperfect.

Even though lab-grown star sapphires and rubies usually have sharper stars and a more intense color than a natural stone, they are not highly valued. They can be found in jewelry supply stores for between $10 and $50 per stone. (However, some of the newer synthetic stones with lighter colors and more natural looking stars sell for a lot more.) In contrast, a natural stone with a similar color and size but a less perfect star than a $30 synthetic stone could sell for several thousand dollars.

Your main concern when judging a star stone should be: is it easy to see the star when you look at the stone under a single, direct light source such as a penlight or light-bulb? (The star will hardly be noticeable in diffuse light from fluorescent lights or overcast skies.) Some secondary questions to ask are:

♦ Is the star centered?
♦ Is the star sharp and well defined?
♦ Are the rays straight?
♦ Are all the rays present?
♦ Do the rays extend completely across the stone?
♦ Is there a good contrast between the star and the background?

Fig. 7.4 A low-priced Indian star ruby with an irregular star

Fig. 7.5 A much more expensive star ruby. Note the sharper star.

Fig. 7.6 Synthetic star sapphire. Note how long and sharp the rays are.

Ideally you should be able to answer yes to all of the preceding questions. In actuality, however, the stars on natural stones tend to be slightly wavy, a little blurry and/or incomplete. Quite often the better the color is, the more imperfect the star looks. Appraisers normally indicate the degree to which the stars conform to the above standards. Under the category of star centering, for example, they may indicate poor, fair, good, very good or excellent.

The degree of transparency also plays a major role in determining the value of star gems. As a general rule, the more transparent a star stone is, the greater its value. A translucent Indian star ruby, for example, may sell for ten times more than if it were opaque.

The evaluation of color in star stones is similar to that of faceted stones, but the overall grading is more lenient. Generally, the more saturated and pure the body color, the more valuable the stone is. Medium and medium-dark tones tend to be the most prized. Light tones, however, are considered acceptable. Natural star sapphires other than the black variety tend to be light blue or gray.

It's normal for star stones to have flaws. However, the more obvious these flaws are to the naked eye, the lower the value of the stone. It's usually best to avoid stones with a lot of surface cracks because they may not be very durable, and they may be dyed.

Star gems have often been worn as good-luck charms. In his book, *The Curious Lore of Precious Stones*, George Kunz states that the three cross-bars of the star were thought to represent faith, hope and destiny. Supposedly, star sapphires were so powerful at warding off bad omens that they would exercise their good influence over their first owners even after passing into other hands. Even today, star stones are worn for good luck, and they are still available. However, don't expect natural star stones to have perfect clarity, symmetry and stars. To find a stone that meets these criteria, consider buying a synthetic stone.

8

Treatments

I f the supply of gems were limited to those specimens that are naturally attractive, they'd be so expensive that most of us could never own them. Therefore, many gems are treated. A **treatment** is any process such as heating, oiling, irradiation, waxing, dying or bleaching which alters the color or clarity of a gem.

Enhancement is often used as another word for treatment. However, it has a broader meaning. "Enhancement" also refers to the faceting and polishing of a gem. In addition, it sounds more positive, which can lead buyers to believe that treatments are always beneficial when they aren't. If stones are improperly heated, for example, they may become brittle, causing them to abrade more easily. Some treatments are not stable. To avoid any misunderstandings, this book normally uses the term "treatment."

Gem Treatments

Heat Treatment: For centuries, gems have been heated to improve their color. However, in the past 30 years, heat treatment has been conducted on a wider scale and at much higher temperatures—1600°C (2900°F) and above. Besides lightening or darkening the color of a stone, heat can improve its clarity. Unless a receipt or lab document states otherwise, you should assume that the following gemstones have probably been heat-treated: aquamarine, carnelian, ruby, sapphire, tanzanite, pink topaz, green tourmaline and blue zircon.

Heat treating is widely accepted because it's a continuation of a natural process and it causes a permanent improvement of the entire stone. From the standpoint of value, it doesn't matter whether commercial-quality stones have been treated or not as long as the color is permanent. The overall quality of the treated stone determines the price. However, a premium may be charged for high-quality *untreated* stones that come with a lab report stating there is no evidence of heat treatment.

If heat treatment is not handled properly, stones may become brittle and therefore less durable. When buying a ruby or a sapphire, for example, check to see if the stone has severe abrasions and pits. Because of their hardness, such stones should normally provide good wear. However, if the stone you're considering has never been worn and most of the facet edges are abraded, it might have a durability problem caused by improper heating.

Irradiation: Various types of radiation are used to intensify or change the color of certain gems. Gamma rays from a cobalt or cesium source are the preferred irradiation agent because they don't induce radioactivity. Pink tourmaline is one example of a stone that is commonly treated with gamma radiation to intensify its color. Untreated pink and red tourmaline owe their color to natural radiation. The gamma treatment merely speeds up the natural process of making colorless tourmaline pink or red. The strength of the color can be a measure of the dose of radiation the stone received naturally and/or through treatment. The color is relatively stable, but strong heat from lights, for example, may sometimes cause it to fade. Fortunately, irradiation treatment will bring back the color. Irradiated pink and red tourmalines are free of radioactivity because the gamma treatment does not change the nuclei of their atoms. Instead, some of the outer electrons are moved to different positions, creating what are called *color centers* which change the way the stone absorbs light.

Topaz is another example of a stone that is routinely irradiated. But in order to obtain the desirable intense blue color, the irradiation is done by one of three different processes. In most cases, colorless topaz is irradiated in a high-energy electron-beam linear accelerator and/or nuclear reactor, which usually turns it brown. The topaz is then heat-treated to produce the stable blue color. The irradiation uses much higher energy levels than that for red tourmaline. This can result in a change to the nucleus of the atoms of impurities in the topaz, creating radioactivity. It may take a few days to many years for the radioactivity to decay. There have been a few isolated cases where blue topaz was sold before it was safe, particularly in the 1980's. In many countries, treated gems are now regulated and must meet certain standards. The United States has the strictest requirements. When suppliers of blue topaz guarantee that their stones come from a licensed facility that's in compliance with standards set by the Nuclear Regulatory Commission, you need not worry about radioactivity in topaz.

Only certain other gem varieties can be enhanced with irradiation. They include:

Maxixe- (ma SHE she) **type beryl**—dark blue beryl from pale pink or colorless beryl; fades
Yellow beryl—from colorless beryl; stable
Smoky quartz—from colorless quartz (rock crystal); stable
Yellow or orange sapphire—from colorless and light yellow sapphire; some fades very quickly,
    some is stable. Most yellow sapphire is heat treated, not irradiated
Diamonds that are green, blue, yellow or brown—from light yellow or brown diamond; stable
"Black" or **Dark-Color Pearls**—from off-color bleached pearls; stable, after a slight fading just
    after treatment

The information on radiation treatment in this section comes primarily from the book *Gemstone Enhancement* by Dr. Kurt Nassau and from personal communication with Dr. Horst Krupp and Dr. Nassau, both physicists, mineralogists and gemologists.

Fracture Filling: If surface fractures in gems are filled with an appropriate substance, the fractures are less noticeable and the overall color and transparency may improve. Emeralds typically have small surface-reaching cracks so they are commonly oiled or filled with an epoxy. Unfortunately, the filling can evaporate over time and sometimes may leave a white or brown residue. This is not a major problem if the stone has been oiled because the stone can be cleaned out by repeated immersion in a solvent such as lacquer thinner. Afterwards it can be re-oiled to look as good as when it was bought. Some epoxy fillings, however, are difficult or impossible to extract. As a result, oiled emeralds are usually preferred over those with epoxy fillings.

Ruby is another stone that may be oiled or filled with epoxy. Glass fillings may also be present in some rubies. During heat treatment, a borax solution used on the stones can melt and form a glass that seeps into fractures and cavities. This improves the stones' appearance.

Emerald oiling is an approved trade practice, but dealers and gemologists disagree on the acceptability of ruby fillings. At any rate, unfilled stones are preferred over filled ones.

Dyeing: Rubies, emeralds, jade and other stones that may have small surface cracks are occasionally dyed with colored oils, epoxies or dyes, especially if they are of very low quality. Some gemstones like lapis lazuli, chalcedony and agate don't need surface cracks to accept dye. They are naturally porous and often dyed. Black onyx is just dyed chalcedony.

Dyed lapis and dyed chalcedony are accepted in the trade, but dyed rubies, emeralds and jade are not. There's nothing wrong with dyed stones as long as you're informed that they're treated and told how to care for them. Dye treatments provide a practical means of making low-grade stones look better. Unfortunately, these stones are often sold with the intent of fooling buyers. Then, instead of being a legitimate treatment, dyeing becomes a deceptive practice.

Surface Diffusion: This treatment is most often done to turn pale or colorless sapphires blue. It may also be used to turn stones red, orange or yellow, or to form a star. The pale stones are packed in chemical powders which impart color and then heated to 1700°C and above until a thin layer of color covers their surface.

Surface diffusion is relatively new (about 25 years old, according to patent records) and is not yet very well accepted by the trade. It is becoming more prevalent, though, and is used on sapphire and ruby that does not respond to standard heat treatment. The color is permanent, but remains only on the surface of the stone. Consequently, the color can be polished or scraped off, leaving the grey or white interior exposed. Some people sell diffusion-treated stones openly, but others try to pass them off as nontreated.

Impregnation and Coating with Wax or Plastic: The ancient Romans used to wax their marble statues to hide cracks and to make the surface look shiny. Today gems are waxed and plasticized for the same reasons. Impregnation can also improve durability and color. Some of the stones that undergo this treatment are turquoise, jade, lapis, malachite and amazonite.

The treating of gemstones is one of the most controversial subjects in the gem trade. Most gem and jewelry organizations now encourage their members to disclose treatments; unfortunately, suppliers don't always tell jewelers how their stones have been treated, so retailers may not have adequate information to pass on to customers. Furthermore, detecting or identifying treatments is not easy. Even the world's foremost gem laboratories find this difficult and sometimes impossible. Nevertheless, jewelers and salespeople should be able to give you general information about gem treatments. For example, they should know that emeralds are usually treated with oil or other fillers to improve their clarity, and they should tell you this. They should also be able to explain to you why emeralds need special attention and how you should care for them. In most cases, however, it's not possible for sellers to know what kind of filler was used and to what extent the filling changed the clarity of the stone. To get more detailed information about a specific stone, you normally have to send it to a gem laboratory. This is advisable if you're buying an expensive gem.

If you don't know a salesperson, it's hard for you to tell if he or she is knowledgeable and ethical. One way of learning something about the character of sellers is to ask what kinds of treatments their stones have undergone. If they're candid and informed, this is a good sign. Reputable salespeople give their customers practical advice and basic facts about gem treatments.

9

Synthetic Stones

To the average person on the street, a synthetic is a fake. In the jewelry trade, though, the word **synthetic** is used differently. It describes a gemstone made in a lab which has the same basic chemical composition and similar chemical, optical and physical properties to its natural counterpart. **A natural gemstone** comes from the ground and is a product of nature, not of man. **Imitations**, on the other hand, do not have the same chemical composition as the stones they resemble, and they may be made by nature or by man. Red glass, for example, can be a man-made imitation of ruby. Garnets used to mimic rubies would be natural imitations.

Since consumers tend to interpret the word "synthetic" differently than jewelers, people who sell synthetic stones usually prefer to describe them with terms such as **created, lab-grown** or **man-made**. Gemologists and natural stone dealers usually identify lab-grown stones as synthetics.

Cultured is sometimes used as a synonym for "lab-grown." The two terms, however, are not equivalent. Culturing pearls is a more natural process than growing gems. A cultured pearl has a nacre coating that is grown in a natural organism and secreted by a natural organism. Man just inserts the irritant into the mollusk. On the other hand, created gems are grown in a lab, not in a natural environment such as the ground, and the chemical ingredients are supplied by man, not by nature through a natural process. It's unfair to the pearl industry and confusing to the public when producers of synthetic gems falsely equate growing gemstones to culturing pearls. This has led many salespeople and consumers to believe cultured pearls are grown in a laboratory when in fact they grow in oysters or mussels in lakes, bays, gulfs, etc.

Synthetic gems are not just a recent phenomenon. Lab-grown ruby, the first synthetic, has been sold commercially since the early 1900's; if your grandmother has some ruby jewelry, the stones could very well have been made in a laboratory. Today, lab-grown stones are even more common, especially in birthstone jewelry and class rings. Synthetics are also found in designer jewelry, set with diamonds in gold or platinum. Some of the stones that are synthetically produced and sold to consumers in jewelry are:

Synthetic alexandrite

Synthetic beryl (red & yellow)

Synthetic chrysoberyl

Synthetic emerald

Synthetic opal

Synthetic quartz (e.g. amethyst & citrine)

Synthetic ruby

Synthetic sapphire

Synthetic spinel

Synthetic turquoise

Some stores call imitation stones "synthetic." For example, imitation tanzanite may be sold as "synthetic tanzanite" because "synthetic" sounds better than "imitation." Green CZ (cubic zirconia) is often called synthetic emerald. Green CZ is a lab-grown stone, but it's not synthetic emerald. It's synthetic CZ, which is much cheaper than lab-grown emerald. The retail price difference between the two stones can be over $150 per carat.

Synthetic Versus Natural

Both natural and synthetic stones of the same gem variety have essentially the same chemical composition, hardness, luster and refractive qualities. However, there will be some important commercial differences, namely:

Price: Most lab-grown stones cost much less than their natural counterparts. The price is determined by their availability, the process used to grow them and market competition.

When lab-grown ruby first appeared on the market, it cost about as much as natural ruby. Today you can buy the same type of lab-grown ruby for less than a couple of dollars a carat. When well-cut, it can be quite attractive. Some synthetic rubies which are grown by a different process may retail for over $300 per carat. This is still much less than if they were natural and had the same color and clarity.

Appearance: One of the biggest advantages of lab-grown stones is that they look attractive and expensive, yet they are normally a lot more affordable than high-quality natural stones.

Rarity: Lab-grown stones can be produced in whatever quantities are needed. As a result, they are readily available. High quality natural stones may be rare and therefore valuable. Finding a good-quality natural stone in the size or shape you'd like is often difficult. You may have to compromise on size, quality, or color.

Emotional Value: Natural gemstones have traditionally had an aura of mystery due to their long, intriguing history and the remote places in which they are mined. Consumers interested in the romantic aspects of gems will generally attach a greater emotional value to a natural stone than one created quickly in a laboratory. To them, there may be no substitute for the "real thing."

Potential for Price Appreciation: Despite market fluctuations, the overall value of natural gems has usually increased over the years. As a result, some have been accepted as a medium of exchange and as collateral for loans. Created gems have not enjoyed this prestige. Instead, their price has generally gone down as production and competition have increased. Rather than being viewed as a portable treasure, synthetic stones are considered an affordable alternative to the natural stone.

Some people may ask, "Why did scientists have to complicate the gem business by creating synthetics?" It's true that synthetic stones have been used to deceive people, and the process of identification has become more complicated. But there's a positive side, too. Thanks to lab-grown stones, people who can't afford certain natural gems are still able to own stones such as good-quality, synthetic rubies and emeralds. Synthetic gem material also benefits industry by being used in lasers, machinery, jets, communication devices, etc. In fact, it's industrial needs that spurred research into the development of synthetic gems.

The next time you admire an attractive gem that's beyond your budget, ask if it's available as a synthetic. If it is, this may be good option for you. Your friends probably won't know the difference; they'll just compliment you on your good taste in gems and wonder how you could afford them.

10

Deceptive Practices

There is no fraud or deceit in the world which yields greater gain and profit than that of counterfeiting gems. (Pliny the Elder, Roman scholar, from his *37th Book of the Historie of the World, 1st century AD*)

Unfortunately, the counterfeiting of gems is as widespread as ever. Today, there are just more ways of doing it. In Pliny's day, there were no lab-grown gemstones. Irradiation and diffusion treatments were unknown. There's nothing wrong with creating synthetics or treating gems. Fraud occurs when a customer is not told that his stone is synthetic or treated.

Listed below are practices that are normally done with the intent to deceive. All of them, however, can be considered legitimate when they are properly disclosed to buyers.

Coating with Colored Substances: Colorless or pale colored stones are sometimes coated with colored plastic. Green plastic coatings are used to make colorless beryl look like emerald and light green jade like valuable imperial jade. Rock crystal coated with red plastic resembles ruby. Occasionally, transparent metallic coatings, like those on modern camera lenses, are applied to colorless gems to add color or brilliance. Varnish and lacquer coatings may also be used. One noteworthy case occurred in 1983 when a 9.58-carat diamond was put up for sale at a major auction in New York. It was supposed to be a fancy pink diamond valued at $500,000. Someone managed to switch it with a light yellow diamond coated with pink nail polish that was worth about one fourth of the appraised value. The deception was discovered a day before the sale.

Painting: You don't have to cover a pale stone with a colored coating to make it look colorful. A little paint in the right spot(s) can do the job. Due to the multiple reflections in a faceted transparent gem, a dab or two of paint on the bottom and/or edge of the stone can make it appear evenly colored when viewed face up. The paint can be hidden by the mounting. Emeralds have at times been colored in this manner. Translucent opal cabochons may be painted on the bottom to enhance and intensify their play of color. Peacock feathers, multi-colored butterfly wings and mother of pearl have on occasion been placed behind opal to improve color play too. Sometimes purple ink is applied on the back of yellowish diamonds or under the prongs of the setting to make the diamonds appear almost colorless and more valuable. Since purple is the complimentary color of yellow, it has the effect of absorbing part of the yellow color. As a result, **beware of closed-back settings**. The bottom of the stone may be painted.

Foil Backing: For probably 4000 years, foil backings have been used to add color and brilliance to gems. As gem-cutting techniques progressed and brought out more brilliance in stones, these backings became less popular. Today foil backings are occasionally found on genuine stones, but they are more likely to be seen on glass imitations. Again, **beware of closed-back settings.** Something such as foil may be concealed underneath the stones, particularly if they are unusually bright. Foil-backed stones are commonly found in antique pieces. The price of this jewelry should be based on its antique value.

Quench Crackling: Stones that are quench crackled have been heated and then plunged into cold water. This procedure is done to produce cracks in synthetic stones so they'll look more natural. Sometimes oil or other liquids are forced into the cracks to imitate the fingerprint inclusions found in natural gems. Colorless quartz may be quench crackled so it can afterwards be fracture-filled with colored oil or dyes and used to imitate emerald or ruby.

Making Composite Stones (Assembled Stones): Stones formed from two or more parts are called **composite** or **assembled stones.** If they're composed of two parts, they're **doublets.** Those consisting of three parts are **triplets.** Assembled opals are one of the most typical composite stones. Opal doublets and triplets are normally disclosed and sold in a legitimate manner so selling them is **not** considered a deceptive practice. Sapphire and ruby doublets, however, are generally used to trick buyers.

Listed below are various types of assembled stones that are sold on the market:

♦ **Natural stone + natural stone of the same gem species:** Natural stones may be glued together for a couple of reasons. One large stone (especially if it's over 1 carat) can be sold for a higher per carat price than two smaller ones. Also, composite stones may have a more valuable color than their individual parts. For example, pale yellow sapphire pieces may be cemented with a blue glue to form a blue sapphire, or opal with a play of color may be glued to common opal.

♦ **Natural stone + synthetic stone of the same gem species:** This is one of the most common types of composite stones. When examined under magnification, it may appear completely natural due to the presence of natural inclusions. The pavilion may be, for example, a deep blue synthetic sapphire, and the crown might consist of pale natural sapphire. The resulting stone is deep blue. Ruby doublets with a synthetic ruby pavilion and a thin natural sapphire crown are quite common.

♦ **Natural stone + glass or a different stone:** One of the best known composite stones is the garnet and glass doublet. It was invented in the mid 1800's to imitate gems of every color. It's a more suitable imitation than glass because the garnet crown is more durable and adds luster to the stone. If you own or have an interest in antique jewelry, you should be especially aware of these doublets. Many of the expensive-looking stones in antique pieces (especially those of the latter half of the 19th century) are nothing but garnet and glass doublets. Today garnet and glass doublets are rare. Glass has also been glued to other stones such as quartz and tanzanite. Slices of opal may be glued to glass, ironstone or black onyx.

♦ **Natural stone + colored glue or gelatin layer + same or another stone:** In Europe and the British Commonwealth countries, this type of assembled stone is called a doublet or **soudé**

stone (French for "soldered stone)." In the United States, they're often called triplets. An emerald triplet in the U.S., for example, consists of two pieces of pale emerald that are joined together with a green gelatin or cement, which is considered to be the third layer. Jade triplets have also been made. They consist of pale jade that has been hollowed out, filled with a green gel and smaller cabochon and then cemented to a jade back to make it look like expensive green jade.

A thin slice of opal cemented with black glue to another material such as potch opal, chalcedony or glass can resemble black opal. This stone is called an **opal doublet**. If it also has a protective top of colorless quartz or glass, then it is called an **opal triplet**.

The key to identifying a composite stone is to find where its parts have been joined together. This can often be seen by immersing the stone in water (immersion tends to make color differences and the glue layer more obvious). Do not immerse assembled opals in water or other liquids; just look at them from the side. Magnification is another helpful identifying technique. It can reveal separation lines, flattened air bubbles between the parts or swirly areas where the stone has been brushed with glue.

Misnomers

Sometimes gems are sold under misleading names. For example, a garnet may be called an "American ruby" or "Cape ruby" to make it seem more valuable. If a salesperson adds a qualifying word or prefix to a gem name, ask him or her to explain what it means. Some misnomers are:

Japanese amethyst	synthetic amethyst	Swiss lapis	dyed blue jasper
Oriental amethyst	purple sapphire	California moonstone	chalcedony
Ceylon diamond	zircon	Black onyx	dyed chalcedony
Brazilian diamond	colorless topaz	Ceylon opal	moonstone
Herkimer diamond	rock crystal quartz		
Mogok diamond	topaz	Balas ruby	spinel
		Bohemian ruby	rose quartz
Brazilian emerald	green tourmaline	Brazilian ruby	topaz
Evening emerald	peridot	California ruby	garnet
Indian emerald	dyed crackled quartz	Colorado ruby	garnet
Medina emerald	green glass	Siberian ruby	tourmaline
Oriental emerald	green sapphire	Spinel ruby	spinel
Spanish emerald	green glass		
Soudé emerald	green composite stone	Brazilian sapphire	tourmaline or topaz
		Meru sapphire	tanzanite
African jade	translucent green garnet	Oriental sapphire	chrysoberyl
Amazon jade	amazonite feldspar	Spinel sapphire	spinel
Australian jade	chrysoprase	Water sapphire	iolite
Colorado jade	amazonite feldspar		
Indian jade	aventurine quartz	Topaz	citrine quartz
Pikes Peak jade	amazonite feldspar	Madeira topaz	citrine quartz
Oregon jade	dark green jasper	Smoky topaz	smoky quartz
Swiss jade	dyed chalcedony	Spanish topaz	citrine quartz
German lapis	dyed blue jasper		

11

Gemstone Descriptions

T he *Gemstone Buying Guide* is designed to help you evaluate the quality of colored gems. That's why six of the preceding chapters were about gemstone value factors. This chapter will give you some brief information about the history, sources and characteristics of the most important gemstones on the market. Before we begin, here's some basic terminology you should know:

Gemstones often may be identified as a group, species or variety. A **group** is composed of a number of closely related species. "Garnet" is an example of a group name. A **species** name refers to a mineral with a characteristic crystal structure and chemical composition. Grossular is one of the species of the garnet group. Another example of a species is quartz, but there is no quartz group. A **variety** name is normally based on color, transparency or optical effects such as color changes and star patterns; but sometimes it has its origins in early history when chemical analyses and crystal structure determinations did not exist. Tsavorite is a green variety of grossular. Amethyst and rock crystal are varieties of quartz. They both have the same essential chemistry and crystal structure but differ in color.

Trade names are often given to gemstones. "Tsavorite" is a trade name that is shorter and more marketable than "transparent green grossular," which is technically a more correct term. **Misnomers** are names which do not correctly identify a gem. Two examples of misnomers are "Herkimer diamond" for colorless quartz and "Kashmir sapphire" when used for sapphire which is not from Kashmir (true Kashmir sapphires of high quality are sold at premium prices).

Sometimes people classify diamonds, rubies, sapphires and emeralds as **precious** gems and other stones such as garnet or opal as **semi-precious**. This is misleading. Some garnets and opals sell for several thousand dollars per carat. On the other hand, there are a lot of opaque rubies and sapphires that sell for less than $10 a carat. In certain contexts, "precious stone" may refer to any stone that is used as a gem. "Precious topaz" can mean real topaz as opposed to citrine quartz or it can refer to high-quality topaz. Since the terms "precious" and "semi-precious" are so confusing, many experts have recommended that they not be used to classify gems.

Each gem species has characteristics which distinguish it from other species. For easy reference, we'll list some of these characteristics below with their definitions.

Refractive Index (RI): the degree to which light is bent as it passes through the stone. This is measured with an instrument called a refractometer. Most colored gems have RI's that range between 1.43 and 1.98. Diamonds have an RI of approximately 2.42, which means they bend light about 2.42 times more than air does. This also means that light travels 2.42 times more slowly through diamonds than it does through air. As a general rule, the higher the RI is, the greater the potential brilliance of the stone. Other factors such as clarity, cut and color also affect brilliance. There can be some variation in the RI of a species depending on a stone's origin and color. This is due to the presence of impurities, which vary according to the source of the stone. The RI of a species may fall slightly above or below the RI ranges listed in this book.

Specific Gravity (SG): the ratio of a gem's density to the density of water. The higher the SG the greater the density is. The SG of most colored gemstones falls between 2.00 and 4.75.

Hardness: the resistance of a gem to scratching and abrasion. This can be classified using the Mohs scale of hardness. The Mohs scale rates the relative hardness of materials with numbers from 1 to 10. The 10 rating of a diamond is the highest and the 1 of talc is the lowest. The intervals between numbers on the scale are not equal, especially between 9 and 10. Ruby and sapphire rate a 9, but a diamond may be over 100 times harder. Some gems like diamond may even have a directional hardness where one direction or surface is harder than another.

Toughness: the resistance of a gem to breaking, chipping or cracking. This is a different property than hardness. Jade is a relatively soft gem material (6-7), yet it is the toughest.

Cleavage: the tendency for a mineral to split along crystal planes, where the atomic bonding is weak. A gemstone may have one or more directions of cleavage, which are classified as perfect (almost perfectly smooth), distinct or indistinct. Cleavage has a negative impact on toughness.

Crystal System: one of the seven classifications of the internal structure of a crystal. It is based on the symmetry of the crystal structure. The simplest and most symmetrical system is called isometric or cubic. The other six systems in the order of their decreasing symmetry are tetragonal, hexagonal, trigonal, orthorhombic, monoclinic and triclinic. For descriptions and diagrams of the seven crystal systems, consult *Gemstones of the World* by Walter Schumann. This book also provides information on stones not included in the *Gemstone Buying Guide*.

Materials which don't have a crystalline structure (e.g. glass) are called **amorphous.** Some gems such as jade and agate are a group of tiny crystals grown together. These gems are classified technically as aggregates (AGG) and are usually translucent to opaque.

Optic Character: the effect a gem material has on light. If it can split light into two rays, each travelling at different speeds, then it is **doubly refractive (DR).** If it does not polarize (split) light, the stone is **singly refractive (SR).** In a doubly refractive gem, there is either one or there are two directions in which light is not split as it passes through it. In other words, a DR stone will behave as if it is singly refractive in at least one direction. The directions of single refraction are called **optic axes.** If the stone has one direction of single refraction, it is **uniaxial,** if it has two, it is **biaxial.**

Doubly refractive gems will have two RI's if they are uniaxial and three RI's if they are biaxial. The numerical difference between the highest and lowest RI is called the **birefringence** or **birefraction.** When you look through stones with a high birefringence, such as peridot, zircon or calcite, the inclusions and facet edges will appear to be doubled. This book does not provide birefringence data, but it gives the optic sign (+ or -). If a uniaxial gem is positive, the lower RI is constant and the higher variable. A negative sign would indicate the reverse. If a biaxial gem is positive, the intermediate RI is closer to the low RI. If negative, it's closer to the high RI.

Pleochroism: the ability of certain gem materials to exhibit different colors when viewed from different directions under transmitted light. A ruby, for example, may appear purplish red in one direction and orangy-red in another. Since it can show two colors, it is **dichroic.** Stones like tanzanite, which can display three colors, are **trichroic.** The strength of pleochroism can range from very strong to very weak. In pastel and colorless stones, pleochroism may not be visible.

Much of the identification data on the following pages was taken from *Gems* by Robert Webster and the GIA *Gem Reference Guide*. Consult these two sources for further information.

Below is a chart which lists the gems in this chapter in the order in which they are presented. It indicates if their name is a group, species or variety classification.

Group	Species	Varieties
None	Chrysoberyl	Alexandrite, cat's-eye, yellow, green or brown (chrysoberyl)
Quartz	Crystallized quartz	Amethyst, ametrine, citrine, hawk's-eye, quartz cat's-eye, rock crystal, rose quartz, smoky quartz, tiger's-eye
Quartz	Cryptocrystalline / microcrystalline quartz (chalcedony)	Agate, bloodstone, carnelian, chalcedony, chrysocolla quartz, chrysoprase, jasper, onyx, plasma, sard
Beryl	Beryl	Emerald, green beryl, aquamarine, Maxixe beryl, heliodor, morganite, goshenite, bixbite, cat's-eye beryl
Garnet	Andradite, spessartine, pyrope almandine, grossular	Demantoid, topazolite, melanite, rhodolite, hessonite, tsavorite, malaia, mali garnet
None	Cordierite	Iolite
Pyroxene	Jadeite (jade)	Green, lavender, "red," gray or white (jadeite)
Amphibole	Actinolite/tremolite (jade)	Nephrite, green, black, brown or white (nephrite)
Sodalite	Lazurite	Lapis lazuli
None	Malachite	
Feldspar	Microcline, orthoclase, albite, oligoclase, labradorite	Moonstone, amazonite, sunstone
None	Opal	Common, white, black, boulder or fire (opal)
Olivine	Forsterite	Peridot, chrysolite
Pyroxene	Spodumene	Kunzite, hiddenite, green spodumene
None	Corundum	Ruby, sapphire, padparadscha, star ruby, star sapphire
Spinel	Spinel	Red, pink, orange, blue or star (spinel)
Epidote	Zoisite	Tanzanite, thulite, green zoisite
None	Topaz	Pink, red, yellow, orange, blue, green or colorless (topaz)
Tourmaline	Elbaite, dravite, chrome dravite, schorl	Green, pink, red, yellow, orange, blue, watermelon, colorless, cat's-eye, bi-color (tourmaline), indicolite
Turquoise	Turquoise	
None	Zircon	Blue, green, red, yellow, orange or brown (zircon)

Alexandrite & Other Chrysoberyls BeAl$_2$O$_4$—Beryllium aluminum oxide

Alexandrite—Alternate birthstone for June; Cat's-eye—18th wedding anniversary stone.

Alexandrite and cat's-eye look very different, yet they are the same mineral—chrysoberyl. A less expensive type of chrysoberyl is transparent, shows no optical effects and ranges in color from green, to yellow to brown. Thanks to their good hardness and durability, chrysoberyls are well-suited for jewelry use. Today, Brazil and Sri Lanka are the most important sources of chrysoberyls. Deposits are also found in Russia, Tanzania, Zimbabwe, Madagascar and Myanmar (Burma). Listed below are the physical and optical characteristics of chrysoberyl:

RI	1.74 - 1.76	Crystal System	Orthorhombic
SG	3.70 - 3.76	Optic Character	DR, biaxial positive
Hardness	8 1/2	Cleavage	Indistinct or none
Toughness	Good to excellent	Stability to Light	Stable
Pleochroism: Strong trichroism in alexandrite, none in cat's-eye, weak to moderate in transparent yellow, green and brown varieties			

ALEXANDRITE: This gem was first discovered in the Ural mountains of Russia in 1830 on the 12th birthday of Czar Alexander II, hence the name. In its finest qualities, alexandrite looks green in sunlight and purplish-red under incandescent light (light bulbs). Coincidentally, red and green were the colors of the Russian Imperial Guard. Don't expect to find natural alexandrite in your local jewelry store—it's very rare. When you do see it for sale, the colors are likely to be a grayish green and brownish purple or lavender. Synthetic alexandrite and synthetic alexandrite-like sapphire or spinel are readily available. Prices for natural alexandrites that show a noticeable change of color start at about $1500 per carat retail and can go over $20,000 per carat depending on size and quality. The distinctness of the color change and the color intensity are the most important price factors, but size and clarity also affect the cost.

CAT'S-EYE: Treasured for centuries in the Orient, cat's-eye became popular in Europe in the late 19th century when the Duke of Connaught gave a cat's-eye engagement ring to Princess Louise Margaret of Prussia. Today, cat's-eye is used mostly in men's jewelry. Other minerals such as quartz, tourmaline and beryl may also display a cat's-eye (stripe of reflected light across a cabochon), but chrysoberyl cat's-eye is the most prized and has the sharpest eye. The unmodified term **cat's-eye** means chrysoberyl cat's-eye. Other cat's-eye stones must indicate the mineral, as for example, cat's-eye quartz or quartz cat's-eye. A brownish yellow similar to the color of honey is the most valued color, but greenish-yellow stones can also be very expensive. In the finest qualities, cat's-eye can wholesale for over $3000 per carat. Stones with fuzzy, non-sharp eyes, dull colors and eye-visible inclusions can sell for less than $100 per carat. Cat's-eye can also display a color change. Alexandrite cat's-eyes, however, are quite rare.

YELLOW, GREEN or BROWN (transparent) **CHRYSOBERYL:** Attractive and durable, high-quality yellow or green chrysoberyl is affordably priced between $100 and $500 per carat, depending on size. Unfortunately, you won't find it in many jewelry stores.

Fig. Al.1 A 2.23 carat Russian alexandrite of unusually fine quality. Viewed under incandescent light, it appears reddish. *Stone courtesy Andrew Sarosi; photo by Robert Weldon.*

Fig. Al.2 The same stone viewed under fluorescent light looks green. It's rare for alexandrite to show such a distinct color change. (Printed colors only approximate actual colors.) *Stone courtesy Andrew Sarosi; photo by Robert Weldon.*

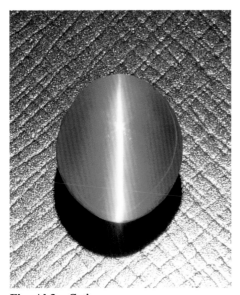

Fig. Al.3 Cat's-eye

Fig. Al.4 Yellow and brownish-orange chrysoberyl

Amethyst & Other Quartz Stones   SiO$_2$—silica (crystallized quartz)

Amethyst—February birthstone and 6th wedding anniversary stone; Citrine—alternate birthstone for November and 13th wedding anniversary stone

Throughout history, supernatural powers have been ascribed to amethyst, rock crystal and other quartz stones. Amethyst, supposedly, could prevent drunkenness and protect people from contagious diseases. Rock crystal spheres have been used to foretell the future. Quartz does in fact have properties that make it seem magical. When quartz crystals are squeezed, they become electrically charged. And if you run an electrical current through a piece of quartz, the crystal will vibrate at a single, constant frequency which is determined by the thickness of the crystal and the strength of the current. This is why synthetic quartz crystals are used to regulate watch movements and the electronic frequencies of radios.

Quartz may be the oldest gemstone known to man. In Europe, rock crystal objects have been unearthed with the remains of prehistoric man (20,000 BC). Archaeologists have found amethyst beads, seals and good luck charms in Egypt which date back to before 3100 BC.

Due to their abundance, quartz gemstones are quite affordable. Amethyst, the most expensive variety, might retail from $2 to $100 per carat depending on quality and cut. Even amethysts that sell for $15 per carat can look good. Mineralogists classify amethyst as a variety of **crystalline** or **crystallized quartz**—quartz which occurs as regular crystals or as coarse aggregates—clusters of crystals that are often visible to the naked eye. Quartz may also be composed of crystals so tiny they can only be seen if you view a thin slice of the stone under high magnification and polarized light. This quartz is called **chalcedony** or more technically **cryptocrystalline** or **microcrystalline quartz**. Chalcedony is discussed in a separate section. Crystallized quartz (generally referred to as simply quartz) has the following properties.

RI	1.544 - 1.553 (very constant)	Crystal System	Trigonal
SG	2.64 - 2.66	**Cleavage**	4 good cleavages
Hardness	7	**Toughness**	Good
Optic Character: DR uniaxial positive or AGG (depending on variety)			
Pleochroism: Weak to moderate. Rock crystal and aggregates show none.			
Reaction to Heat: Strong heat may change the color of amethyst, rose quartz and smoky quartz. Sudden temperature changes can cause fracturing or cleaving.			
Stability to Light: Some rose quartz and amethyst may fade.			

Quartz Varieties & Trade Names

AMETHYST (Purple or violet quartz): The most expensive color is an intense, deep, evenly-colored purple with flashes of red under incandescent light, and the least costly is pale lavender. Transparent, high clarity stones are readily available at low prices. Four major sources of amethyst are Brazil, Uruguay, Bolivia and Zambia. A lot of synthetic amethyst, citrine and other colors of synthetic quartz are made in Japan and especially in Russia. Some amethyst is heat-

Fig. Am.1 85-carat ametrine briolette. *Courtesy Cynthia Renée Co.; photo by Colladay.*

Fig. Am.2 Rock crystal dancer with opal and diamond accents. Designed and carved by Peggy Croft. *Photo by Harold & Erica Van Pelt.*

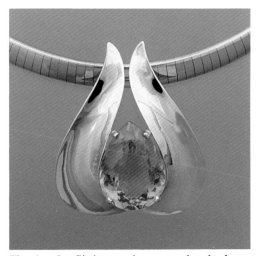

Fig. Am.3 Citrine pendant created and photographed by Linda Quinn

Fig. Am.4 Flower pins carved from aventurine and rose quartz

treated to lighten its color or to transform it into citrine and sometimes green quartz. Green and yellow quartz can be irradiated to produce amethyst. The color of amethyst can fade from heat treatment or long exposure to sunlight.

AMETRINE (Purple- and yellow-zoned quartz, i.e. amethyst + citrine): This popular gem is mined commercially in Bolivia and has only been available since the late 1980's. Its two colors allow cutters to create stones and sculptures with striking zonal patterns.

AVENTURINE: A translucent to opaque rock called quartzite (technically, a polycrystalline aggregate of quartz grains) with a glittery effect often caused by mica inclusions. Aventurine is typically green, but it may also be gray, yellow or brown.

CITRINE (Yellow or orange quartz): Most citrine is heat-treated amethyst or smoky quartz. Natural-color citrine is rare and is usually pale yellow. Its name is derived from the French word for lemon—*citron*. A lot of citrine is sold as topaz.

PRASIOLITE (Green Quartz): This transparent green to yellowish-green quartz has been produced since the early 1950's by heating amethyst. Natural-color prasiolite is extremely rare.

DRUSY QUARTZ: A bed of tiny quartz crystals found in hollow rock cavities. Drusy quartz is sometimes used as a jewelry accent by designers.

QUARTZ CAT'S-EYE: Sri-Lanka, India and Brazil are sources of quartz cat's-eye. It may be white, green, yellow or brown.

ROCK CRYSTAL (Colorless quartz): This is the most widely distributed variety of quartz. Nowadays, the term *crystal* by itself usually means fine-quality glass, but technically it is transparent, colorless quartz. *Crystal* comes from the Greek word for ice. Besides being cut as beads and faceted stones, rock crystal is used for lenses and all sorts of decorative objects. Once in awhile, it is quench-crackled (heated and cooled immediately) and then dyed green or red to imitate emerald and ruby.

ROSE QUARTZ (Pink quartz): This quartz, which is typically translucent, is sometimes irradiated to intensify its color. Occasionally, rose quartz shows a star effect.

RUTILATED QUARTZ: Colorless transparent quartz that has needle-like inclusions of a mineral called rutile.

SMOKY QUARTZ (Brown to black quartz): Even though smoky quartz is found worldwide, some of it on the market is irradiated rock crystal and this tends to be very dark. When it is from the Cairngorm mountains of Scotland, it is called **Cairngorm**. This quartz is often sold incorrectly under the misnomer "smoky topaz."

TIGER'S-EYE: A translucent to opaque quartz with a silky luster and brown and gold stripes. (Technically, it's a quartz replacement of a type of asbestos called crocidolite.) Stones cut *en cabochon* with a gold band along the center resemble a cat's-eye due to the fibrous structure of the stone. South Africa is the most important source of tiger's-eye. A grayish-blue quartz with a similar cat's-eye effect is called **HAWK'S-EYE**.

Fig. Am.5 Citrine and smoky quartz pendant designed, manufactured and photographed by The Diamond Dove, Inc.

Fig. Am.6 Tiger's-eye cabochon on a flattened tiger's eye oval

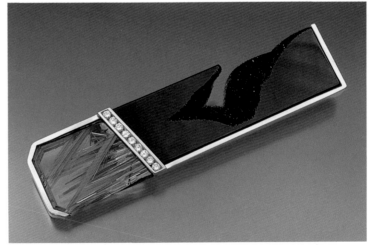

Fig. Am.7 Amethyst pendant created and photographed by Somos Creations.

Fig. Am.8 Brooch made from rutilated quartz and black drusy onyx. *Created and photographed by Linda Quinn.*

Chalcedony SiO_2—Silica (Microcrystalline quartz)

Bloodstone—March Birthstone; Sardonyx—August birthstone; Onyx—7th wedding anniversary

Designers love gem varieties of chalcedony (cal CED nee). Its unique patterns and color combinations allow them to create attractive jewelry pieces that are unique. Chalcedony is affordable, very durable and suitable for fine carving. Besides being used in jewelry, it's also fashioned into bowls, vases, figurines, paper weights and other decorative articles.

Chalcedony is a confusing term because it has three different meanings. It can refer to a species of the quartz group—called microcrystalline or cryptocrystalline quartz (quartz composed of microscopic-size crystals). It can be a *sub*-category of microcrystalline quartz—the type whose crystal components look like sub-parallel to divergent fibers rather than grains like those of many jaspers, and chalcedony can indicate a specific variety of chalcedony that is plain white, gray or bluish gray. Properties of chalcedony are listed below:

RI	1.53 - 1.54	Crystal System	Trigonal
SG	2.58 - 2.64; some jasper up to 2.91	Optic Character	AGG
Hardness	6 1/2 - 7	Cleavage	None
Toughness	Very good	Pleochroism	None
Reaction to Heat: The color may change depending on the cause of color.			
Stability to Light: Usually stable, but stones dyed with organic dyes can fade.			

Varieties & Trade Names

AGATE: Dealers tend to apply the term agate to any patterned chalcedony that is translucent or semi-translucent, as opposed to jasper which is usually opaque to the naked eye. In a more strict usage, agate is a chalcedony with curved or angular bands (layers) of color. The bands may be multicolored or similar in color. Certain types of colorless or gray agates from Brazil and Madagascar are often stained (permanently dyed) red, black, green, blue or yellow with stable, inorganic chemicals. The main cutting and processing center for agate is Idar-Oberstein in Germany, where a lot of agate used to be mined. Now it is shipped there from Brazil and Madagascar. Other sources of agate are the U.S., Mexico, Russia and India.

Some white, gray or colorless chalcedony with inclusions is called agate. **MOSS AGATE** has moss-like green, brown, and/or red inclusions. **DENDRITIC AGATE (LANDSCAPE AGATE)** has dark inclusions that resemble trees or ferns.

Agate formed in cavities may have a crystallized crust of tiny quartz crystals (e.g. geode). This agate is called **DRUSY AGATE** or **DRUSY CHALCEDONY.**

BLOODSTONE (HELIOTROPE): An opaque dark green chalcedony with orange or red spots, which some Christians thought represented the blood of Jesus Christ. Bloodstone used to be prescribed as a cure for all types of bleeding. The injured or sick person would either wear it or place it over the affected area and the bleeding was supposed to stop. India is the main source of bloodstone.

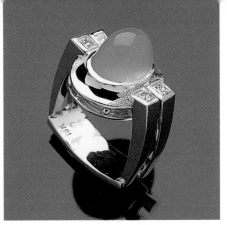

Fig. Ca.8 Chrysoprase ring by Richard Kimball. *Photo by Steve Ramsey*

Fig. Ca.9 Left, jasper brooch; right, agate brooch

Fig. Ca.10 Dinosaur-bone pendant. *Design by Lori Braun; jewelry and photo copyright by Murphy Design.*

Fig. Ca.11 Jasper earrings. *Design by Lori Braun; jewelry and photo copyright 1995 by Murphy Design.*

Fig. Ca.12 Carnelian

Fig. Ca.13 Picture jasper from Idaho

Emerald & Other Beryl Stones Be$_3$Al$_2$(SiO$_3$)$_6$—Beryllium aluminum silicate

Emerald—May birthstone; aquamarine—March birthstone; emerald—20th & 35th anniversary

In its pure form, beryl is colorless. But thanks to the presence of impurities, this mineral can be blue, green, pink, red, yellow or orange. If, for example, traces of chromium and/or vanadium are present, the result may be an emerald. A trace of iron can turn the beryl into an aquamarine, whereas a bit of manganese adds a pink or orange color to the stone.

Of all the beryls, emerald is the most highly valued and has the longest history. Some evidence indicates that emerald deposits in Egypt may have been exploited as early as 3500 BC. However, most of the Egyptian emeralds were pale, drab and heavily flawed. It wasn't until the 1500's, when the Spanish invaded the Americas, that Europeans realized how beautiful an emerald could be and vast quantities of Colombian emeralds were brought to Europe by the conquistadors.

Aquamarine and yellow beryl have also had a long history, but it's hard to determine when they were first used. The orange, pink and red beryls have only been recognized as gems since the early 1900's. Listed below are the physical and optical properties of the beryl family.

RI	1.57 - 1.60	**Crystal System**	Hexagonal
SG	2.67 - 2.80	**Optic Character**	DR, uniaxial negative
Hardness	7 1/2 - 8	**Cleavage**	Rare and indistinct in one direction

Toughness: Poor to good depending on clarity

Pleochroism: Emerald, moderate to strong yellowish-green and bluish-green; weak to moderate dichroism in the other beryls

Reaction to Heat: In emerald, it may cause fracturing or complete breakage; Maxixe and Maxixe-type beryl fade quickly at 100^0 C or higher.

Reaction to Chemicals: Resists all acids except hydrofluoric; solvents such as acetone and alcohol may drive out fracture fillings in emerald.

Stability to Light: Stable, except for Maxixe and Maxixe-type beryl. There can also be fading in orange beryl or in emeralds treated with green oil. In addition, orange beryl may change to pink.

Varieties & Trade Names

EMERALD: The definition of an emerald varies depending on the user. At gem shows and in stores, any beryl that looks more or less green is typically labeled as an emerald. Some emerald dealers feel that light green stones should be called "green beryl" and that the term "emerald" should be reserved for darker stones. European mineralogists tend to believe true emeralds must be colored by chromium, whereas American gemologists feel stones colored by vanadium can also be classified as emeralds. The definition of "emerald" is irrelevant when it comes to pricing. If a one-carat beryl has a saturated green color and is transparent and eye-clean, it can be worth over $5000 wholesale. Top quality, 6-carat emeralds can wholesale for over $15,000 **per carat**. If a beryl is light green and has poor transparency, it's not worth much, no matter how it's labeled.

Fig. Em.1 Aquamarine sculpted by Sherris Cottier Shank. *Photo by John McMartin.*

Fig. Em.2 A 4.33-carat Zambian emerald. *Ring and photo Courtesy Color Masters Gem Corp.*

Fig. Em.3 Yellow beryl. *Ring and photo courtesy Robert Trisko Jewelry Sculptures.*

Fig. Em.4 Morganite jewelry. *Gems from Cynthia Renée Co.; jewelry by Nanz Aalund; photo by Jeff Engelstad.*

Low-grade emerald or beryl can sell for as little as $10 per carat. It's normal for an emerald to be flawed with inclusions and cracks, especially if it has a deep green color. Nevertheless, clarity and transparency play a major role in emerald pricing. Emeralds are routinely treated with oil or epoxy substances to hide cracks and improve transparency. This is considered an acceptable trade practice as long as it is disclosed. Some fillers, however, are more preferred than others. Cedarwood oil is considered more stable than palm oil. In expensive emeralds, oil is preferred over epoxy fillers. It's impossible for most salespeople to know what an emerald has been filled with. They should, however, be able to tell you how to care for it. Reputable jewelers will stand behind their emeralds, and many will retreat the stones if necessary. For a fuller discussion of emerald treatments, quality evaluation and identification, consult the *Emerald & Tanzanite Buying Guide* by Renée Newman.

Colombia is the most important source of top-grade emerald. High-quality emerald is also found in Zambia, Zimbabwe, Brazil and Pakistan, but not in the same quantities as in Colombia. Other deposits include Russia, Afghanistan, Australia, India and North Carolina.

GREEN BERYL: There is no agreed-upon criterion in the trade for distinguishing between green beryl and emerald. Likewise, there is no clear dividing line between green beryl and aquamarine.

AQUAMARINE: The name "aquamarine" means "sea water" in Latin, alluding to its color. Most natural-color aquamarine is light bluish-green. Prior to the 1900's, this was the preferred color for the stone. Today aquamarine is routinely heat-treated to remove the green component, thereby producing a permanently-colored blue stone. The more intense the blue color, the more valuable the stone. Aquamarines usually have a high transparency and clarity, even under magnification. In addition, they are very durable and their color is evenly distributed. Brazil is the most important producer of aquamarine. Madagascar, Mozambique, Ukraine, Nigeria, Pakistan and Zambia are other major sources.

MAXIXE BERYL: This beryl has a medium to dark color resembling sapphire. It was named after the mine in Brazil where it was discovered around 1917. Since then, a similar stone has appeared on the market called Maxixe-type beryl. It is produced by irradiating pale pink or colorless beryl. Maxixe and Maxixe-type beryls are rare and they fade when exposed to light.

HELIODOR (YELLOW BERYL): Found in Madagascar, Brazil, Russia, Namibia and the U.S., this beryl is not uncommon. It has also been called golden beryl.

MORGANITE (PINK, ORANGE or PURPLE BERYL): Morganite was named after the famous financier J. P. Morgan. The first morganite to be described was a pale pink variety found in California. Some of the finest, most intensely-colored morganite is found in Madagascar. Brazil is another important source, but the colors are usually lighter even though the crystals are much larger. To purify the color, some morganite is heat-treated.

RED BERYL (BIXBITE): This valuable beryl was discovered in Utah in 1906. Red beryl is sometimes erroneously called red emerald. Due to its rarity, it remains a collector gem.

GOSHENITE (COLORLESS BERYL): Goshenite is named after Goshen, Massachusetts, where it was first found. It has been used to imitate diamond or emerald by placing silver or green colored metal foil behind it in a closed back setting. Goshenite is not common.

CAT'S-EYE BERYL: Chatoyancy is most likely to occur in aquamarine and morganite. However, cat's-eye emerald and cat's-eye yellow beryl also exist. These are collector stones.

Fig. Em.6 Colombian emeralds. *Photo and jewelry courtesy Harry Winston, Inc.*

Fig. Em.5 A ring-shaped aquamarine (Torus Ring™) carved and photographed by Glenn Lehrer

Fig. Em.7 Heliodor (yellow beryl)

Fig. Em.8 Maxixe-type beryl. *Photo by Robert Weldon.*

Garnet (a group of gem species)

January birthstone and 2nd wedding anniversary stone

Friendship—this is what the garnet represents. According to legend, adorning yourself with garnets will improve your personal relationships and protect you from harm. These benefits are doubled if your birthday is in January. Traditionally, people have considered garnets to be red, but they can also be various shades of green, yellow, orange, brown, pink or purple.

The word "garnet" comes from the Latin *granatum* meaning "seedlike." Garnet crystals in rock reminded early scientists of the shape and color of pomegranate seeds.

Historical accounts and findings suggest that garnet beads and inlaid jewelry were worn in Egypt as early as 3100 BC. Tracing the history of gemstones is difficult because they were often misidentified. It's certain, though, that during the 18th and 19th centuries, garnets were popular in Europe. The bourgeoisie would buy these stones while vacationing in the hot springs of Bohemia, Czechoslovakia, and take them home as souvenirs and good luck charms. Until the late 1800's, Bohemia was the world's major source of pyrope garnet (a garnet species).

Below is a chart which lists various members of the garnet group. Much of the data is from *Gems* by Robert Webster. Keep in mind that garnets are almost always a mixture of different garnet species and have varying properties. The species name refers to the main component of a garnet. Use this table as a general guide only; the RI, SG and hardness values may be higher or lower than indicated, and there can be a wide variation of color within a given species. One garnet species, uvarovite, was not included because it's too rare and small to be of value for jewelry use.

Species	Varieties	Basic Color	RI	SG	Hardness
Andradite	Demantoid Topazolite Melanite	Green Yellow / orange Black	1.88 - 1.89	3.81 - 3.87	6 1/2 - 7
Spessartine		Orange	1.79 - 1.81	4.12 - 4.20	7 1/4
Almandine (if pure) Almandine		Purple Purple	1.83 1.78 - 1.83	4.25 3.95 - 4.25	7 1/2 7 1/4
Pyrope-almandine	Rhodolite	Purple-red / pink	1.75 - 1.78	3.80 - 3.95	7 1/4
Pyrope Pyrope (if pure)		Red Red	1.73 - 1.75 1.71	3.65 - 3.80 3.51	7 1/4 7 1/4
Grossular-andradite	Mali garnet	Green or yellow	1.75 - 1.78	3.64 - 3.68	
Pyrope-spessartine	Color change & Malaia garnet	Variable Orange / pink-orange	1.74 - 1.78	3.78 - 3.85	7 1/4
Grossular	Hessonite Tsavorite Translucent green Translucent white Translucent pink	Orange or yellow Green Green White Pink	1.74 - 1.76 1.74 - 1.76 1.72 - 1.73 1.72 - 1.73 1.70 - 1.73	3.59 - 3.65 3.57 - 3.64 3.42 - 3.50 3.45 - 3.50 3.35 - 3.41	7 1/4 7 1/4 7 7 7

Fig. G.1 Demantoid garnet ring from Cynthia Renée Co. *Photo by Robert Weldon.*

Fig. G.2 A 4.48 ct-spessartite garnet flanked by two tsavorites. *Ring by Gary Dulac; photo copyright 1994 by Azad.*

Fig. G.3 Malaya garnet ring made and photographed by Libby Skamfer

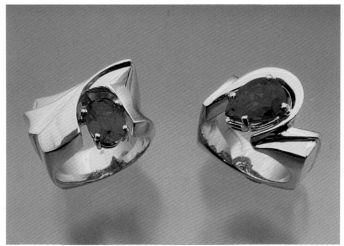

Fig. G.4 Rhodolite rings created and photographed by Linda Quinn.

Jewelers normally identify lower priced garnets as simply garnets. It's not worth the time and money to test the stones and determine their species category. Properties shared by the various garnets are listed below.

Crystal System	Cubic (isometric)	Toughness	Fair to good
Optic Character: Singly refractive, anomalous double refraction			
Cleavage: None, but may have indistinct parting			
Reaction to Heat: Sudden temperature changes tend to cause fracturing			

Species, Varieties & Trade Names

ANDRADITE ($Ca_3Fe_2(SiO_4)_3$): The best known andradite variety is **DEMANTOID**, which was discovered in 1868 in the Ural Mountain area of Russia. It resembles an emerald with added brilliance and fire. Its fire (dispersion) is greater than that of any other natural gemstone, including diamond. Though seldom used today, a lot of Victorian gemstone jewelry made between 1885 and 1915 featured demantoid.

Good demantoid is not easy to find today. For more than 80 years, most of the mining in Russia ceased, but the Russians are now producing it again. Some demantoid is mined in Mexico, Italy, Czechoslovakia and Arizona but the color tends to be yellowish, so it is not as highly prized as that found in Russia. Asbestos-fiber inclusions resembling horsetails are considered a positive feature in demantoid. Their presence strongly suggests the stones are from the Russian Ural region, which has also been the source of some high-quality alexandrite. The retail price of demantoid can range from about $400 to over $5000 per carat.

The opaque black variety of andradite, **MELANITE**, has been used in mourning jewelry. The crystals of **TOPAZOLITE**, another variety, are small and of little importance as gemstones.

SPESSARTINE or **SPESSARTITE** ($Mn_3Al_2(SiO_4)_3$): This variety can be yellowish orange to reddish orange. The most valued color is orange with red overtones. Spessartine is sometimes confused with yellow topaz or hessonite garnet. Sources include Sri Lanka, Brazil, Afghanistan, Myanmar, Madagascar, East Africa and California. One place that's particularly noted for high-quality spessartine is the Little Three Mine in California. Kenya and Brazil also produce some fantastic spessartine. Retail prices of top-grade material can be as high as $1000 per ct. Most spessartines on the market, though, tend to sell for about $5 to $200 per carat.

ALMANDINE or **ALMANDITE** ($Fe_3Al_2(SiO_4)_3$): Much of the material which is sold as almandine is low-priced pyrope (garnet composed mostly of pyrope with some almandine and grossular). This leads people to believe that almandine is more plentiful than it actually is. Opinions differ as to how almandine should be defined. At the very least, the chief component should be almandine. But mineralogists disagree on how much almandine should be present and what its properties should be. According to noted gemologist Robert Webster (*Gems*, p. 174), the bottom limits for the refractive index and specific gravity of almandine are 1.78 and 3.95. However, these figures are arbitrary. Almandines of high purity are rare and typically have a

Fig. G.5 Top left to right: Mali garnet, hessonite. Bottom left to right: spessartine garnet, grossular garnet.

Fig. G.6 Pyrope garnet ring by Dan Miller. *Photo by Luciano Baldi.*

Fig. G.7 Tsavorite garnet. *Ring courtesy Proprioro; photo by TKO Studios.*

purplish color. Sources include Sri Lanka, India, Brazil, Australia, Tanzania, Madagascar and the U.S. Star almandine is found in Idaho. These star garnets usually have four rays but six rays may be seen in certain directions of some stones.

RHODOLITE (Pyrope-almandine): Rhodolite was discovered in 1882 in North Carolina. Those deposits have been depleted, but since then it has been found in Africa, Brazil, India and Sri Lanka. Tanzania is the major commercial source. The name of this purplish-red garnet comes from the Greek *rhodo* (rose) and *lithos* (stone). Rhodolites can range in price from $5 to $400 per carat retail. Top-quality stones are clean, very transparent and saturated in color but not dark.

PYROPE (PIE rope) ($Mg_3Al_2(SiO_4)_3$): This garnet's name is derived from the Greek *pyropos* meaning "fire-like," alluding to its deep red color. Pyrope is found throughout the world, with some of the best quality coming from the diamond mines of South Africa. As a result, it has sometimes been referred to as "cape ruby." "Arizona ruby" is a misnomer for pyrope from Arizona. Pyrope is a very affordable stone with retail prices ranging from about $5 to $100 per carat. The redder the stone, the more valuable it is. Eye-clean material is readily available.

MALI GARNET or **GRANDITE** (Grossular-andradite): Marketed only since 1995, Mali garnets are found in western Africa in the Republic of Mali. They can be various shades of green, yellow or brown. These "new" garnets often resemble faceted chrysoberyl, and their prices are similar.

MALAIA (MALAYA): Consisting mostly of pyrope-spessartine, this distinctive orange variety may be reddish, pinkish or yellowish. It was found in East Africa in the search for rhodolite, a purplish-red garnet coveted in Japan. Pinkish orange and orange with overtones of red are the most valued malaia colors. Top qualities can retail for up to $500 whereas low-grade malaia can sell for as little as $10 per carat. In Europe, gemologists often refer to it as **umbalite**. "Malaia" is the Swahili word for "outcast" or "prostitute."

    COLOR-CHANGE GARNET is found in many different colors and displays a variation of color behavior. For example, it may be blue or green in daylight and red in incandescent light. Color-change garnet consists mainly of pyrope-spessartine with some grossular.

GROSSULAR or **GROSSULARITE** ($Ca_3Al_2(SiO_4)_3$): The most valued variety of this species is **TSAVORITE** (also **tsavolite**), a transparent green garnet. It was discovered in Tanzania in 1968. Later it was also found in Kenya, and promoters from Tiffany & Co. named it after the country's Tsavo National Park. Tsavorite is found in almost all shades of green but tends to be yellowish-green. When its color resembles that of fine emerald, it can wholesale for over $3000 per carat in sizes over 3 carats. Retail prices of smaller commercial quality stones can drop down to $100 per carat.

    HESSONITE is a much less expensive variety of grossular that is sometimes called **cinnamon stone**.   The colors are often brownish and can be red, orange, yellow or colorless. When viewed under magnification, hessonite typically has a granular "heat wave" appearance. There are hessonite deposits in Sri Lanka, the U.S., Canada, Madagascar, Siberia and Brazil.

    Translucent and opaque grossular is used for beads, cabochons and carvings. The green material (technically named **hydrogrossular**) is sometimes called **Transvaal jade**, after its main source in South Africa. It has also been found in the USSR, Hungary and Italy. Small black inclusions (black specks) are a characteristic of this green grossular. Translucent pink grossular, mixed in white marble, is found mainly in Mexico and is sometimes called **rosolite**, after its color.

Iolite (Cordierite species) $Mg_2Al_4Si_5O_{18}$—a complex silicate of magnesium and aluminum

21st wedding anniversary stone

Before the 1980's, iolite was mainly considered a collector's stone because so little of it was being sold. Today, it is more readily available, and it is often used as a sapphire or tanzanite substitute due to its blue-violet color and lower price. You can find high-quality iolite for less than $200 per carat retail. Overly dark and flawed stones sell for much less.

Mineralogists call the stone **cordierite,** a name given to the mineral in honor of French geologist Pierre Cordier. The name iolite was derived from the Greek word for violet, *ios*. Some people have referred to iolite as **water sapphire** because it resembles sapphire face-up and it looks clear or watery from the side. This effect is due to the strong trichroism of iolite. In one direction the crystal typically appears dark blue or violet; in another it is colorless, gray or yellowish; and in a third direction it is light blue or violet.

Iolite has also been referred to as the "Viking's compass." On cloudy days, the Vikings were able to locate the position of the sun by looking through thin colorless slices of iolite. The stone acted as a light polarizer and canceled out haze and mist.

The Vikings probably got their iolite from Greenland or Norway, but today most of it comes from India, Sri Lanka, Tanzania and Brazil. Additional sources include Myanmar, Madagascar, Zimbabwe and Namibia. The physical and optical properties of iolite are listed below.

RI	1.53 - 1.58	**Crystal System**	Orthorhombic
SG	2.56 - 2.66	**Optic Character**	DR, biaxial negative
Hardness	7 - 7 1/2	**Cleavage**	Distinct in one direction
Toughness	Fair	**Pleochroism**	Strong trichroism
Reaction to Chemicals: Attacked by acids			

Fig. I.1 Iolite ring from Proprioro. *TKO studios.*

Fig. I.2 Emerald-cut iolite

Jade (Jadeite & Nephrite)

12th wedding anniversary stone

> *...jade is a possession to be cherished by anyone who can find it or buy it or steal it. Chinese women ask for jade ornaments for their hair, and old men keep in their closed palms a piece of cool jade, so smooth that it seems soft to the touch. Rich men buy jades instead of putting their money in banks, for jade grows more beautiful with age.*
> Pearl S. Buck, *My Several Worlds*

There is no other stone that is as resistant to breakage and chipping as jade. This inherent toughness made it a superior weapon and tool for early man. To him it meant survival, and its colors were reminiscent of nature. As a result, jade became known as a gift from heaven. It was even more esteemed than diamonds or gold by some civilizations in Asia, Central America and the South Pacific.

According to the great Chinese philosopher Confucius, jade was highly valued for a variety of reasons—its polish and brilliancy represent the whole of purity; its compactness and hardness represent the sureness of the intelligence; the pure and prolonged sound which it gives forth when one strikes it represents music; its color represents loyalty (from *Jade: Stone of Heaven* by Richard Gump, pg 23). Today jade is worn by millions of Orientals for good luck and health, and it is given to celebrate all important occasions in life such as births, marriages, anniversaries and business agreements.

The Spanish conquistadors are credited for giving us the term "jade." When they learned that natives in Mexico were wearing jade to relieve kidney ailments, they called it *piedra de ijada* meaning "stone of the loins." Gradually, the Spanish term evolved to "jade." The early Romans had also considered jade to be a good cure for kidney ailments such as nephritis (kidney inflammation) and called jade *lapis nephriticus*—"stone of nephrite." Later the Latin term was reduced to "nephrite" and was used as an alternate word for jade. In 1863, the French chemist Augustine Damour realized that jade was two different minerals, so he coined the word **jadeite** for Burmese jade to distinguish it from Chinese jade—**nephrite**. The Chinese had been aware of the difference between the two jades since the mid 1700's.

Jadeite and nephrite are both rocks (aggregates)—masses of tightly interlocking crystals, rather than single crystals like most gems. However, they have different chemical compositions and properties. Jadeite is a little harder and denser, and as a result can take a higher polish than nephrite. Neither stone is very hard, compared to diamond. ruby and sapphire. However, both jades are unusually tough—resistant to breakage and chipping. Valuable jade carvings, for example, have survived falls in earthquakes when other hard objects nearby have not. Nephrite, however, is slightly stronger, due to its intergrown, fiberlike crystal components. Jadeite is made up of crystals which tend to be more granular and more coarse. These are sometimes visible without magnification.

Jadeite is more valuable and rare than nephrite. Myanmar (Burma) has been the main source of jadeite since the late 18th century, when China began to import jade from there. Prior to that time, Guatemalan jadeite had been used extensively in Central America by Indians such as the Aztecs and the Mayas. Some jadeite is also mined in Russia, Japan and California; but the finest quality comes from Myanmar. When it is very translucent and has a strong emerald-green color, it is often called **Imperial jade**. Jadeite is found in a variety of colors—lavender, white, gray, yellow, orange, brownish-red, black and many shades of green. Today, jadeite is usually the jade chosen for fine jewelry. Its intrinsic value is generally the basis for its price. Nephrite, on the other hand, is mainly valued for its antiquity and carving excellence.

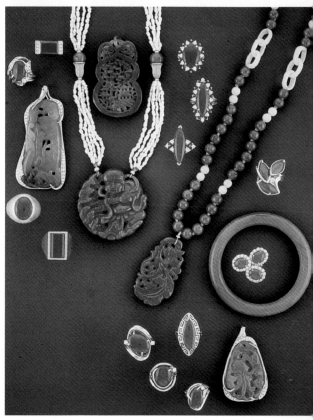

Figs. J.1, J.2 and J.3: Green, "red" and lavender jade pieces. *Jewelry and photographs courtesy Mason-Kay.*

Nephrite is plentiful and most of it is grayish green—typically forest green or olive green. It can also be white, gray, black, brown, yellow or beige. The oldest known source of nephrite is Xinjiang Province in China (formerly Eastern Turkestan). For centuries, this is where China got its jade. The nephrite found in Xinjiang tends to be light in color. Although it is usually thought of as an oriental stone, nephrite was also mined and carved in ceremonial fashion by other cultures throughout history—notably the Maoris of New Zealand. Nephrite is also found in Taiwan, British Columbia, Australia, Poland, Germany, India, Zimbabwe, Mexico, Alaska, California and Wyoming. The chemical composition and properties of nephrite and jadeite can be compared by referring to the two charts below:

Jadeite $NaAl(Si_2O_6)$—Sodium aluminum silicate			
RI	1.66 - 1.68	**Crystal System**	Monoclinic
SG	3.30 - 3.36	**Optic Character**	AGG (DR) biaxial positive
Hardness	6 1/2 - 7	**Toughness**	Exceptional

Nephrite $Ca_2(Mg,Fe)_5(Si_4O_{11})_2(OH)_2$—Calcium magnesium iron silicate			
RI	1.60 - 1.63	**Crystal System**	Monoclinic
SG	2.90 - 3.05	**Optic Character**	AGG (DR) biaxial positive
Hardness	6 - 6 1/2	**Toughness**	Exceptional, even better than jadeite

Evaluation of Jade

Color: An intense green with a medium to medium-dark tone is the most valued. As the color becomes lighter, darker, more grayish or brownish or yellowish, the value decreases. Lavender is the next most valued hue, followed by red, yellow, white and black. Prior to the importation of Burmese jadeite into China, white nephrite was the jade most coveted by Chinese royalty.

Color Uniformity: In top quality jade, the color is uniform throughout the stone. The more uneven or blotchy the color is, the lower the value. Multi-colored jade, however, can be very expensive if the colors are intense and distinct. The most desired color combinations are green and lavender, orange and green, or white with strong green (**moss-in-snow** jade).

Transparency: The best jade is either semi-transparent or highly translucent. In his book *Jade for You*, jade dealer John Ng says jade can even be near transparent. It's called **water jade**, whereas semi-transparent jade is labeled **honey jade**. As the transparency of jade decreases, so does its value, with opaque jade being worth the least. One exception is white jade. Since it's low-priced and readily available in translucent qualities, transparency has little effect on its value.

Many jade dealers use the term **translucency** instead of "transparency." For the sake of consistency, this book uses the term "transparency" when categorizing the degree to which light passes through gems.

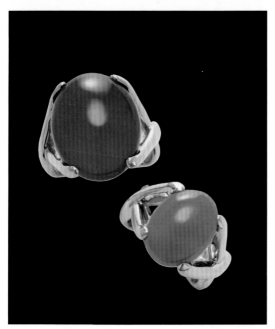

Fig. J.4 Top-quality green and lavender jadeite. Today, fine material like this is cut into cabochons. *Jewelry and photo courtesy Mason-Kay; photo by Richard Rubins.*

Fig. J.5 Spinach jadeite (dark-green jade) skillfully cut into a swan—it was difficult to create such symmetrical veins and feathers. Formerly, jade pieces were often carved for aesthetic reasons; today, they are carved to remove imperfections. Consequently, smooth jade is now more valuable than carved jade. *Courtesy Mason-Kay.*

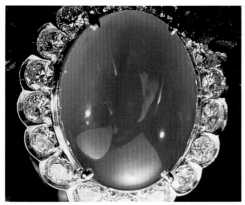

Fig. J.6 This jadeite cabochon is very translucent and has a superb polish, but its color is a little too light for it to qualify as top-quality jade. Nevertheless, the stone wholesaled for $40,000 in 1997. *Courtesy Mason-Kay.*

Fig. J.7 Nephrite jewelry from British Columbia. The dark green jade is a typical nephrite color. The lighter green is not so common and is more in demand in the Orient as a nephrite color.

Clarity: Fine jade is free of flaws such as cracks, included foreign material, cloudy areas, streaks and spots which reduce beauty or durability. The number, size, color, position and nature of flaws determines the clarity of a stone. Fractures that break the surface or that are visible internally are particularly detrimental to the value of jade.

Texture: Jade can have a texture that ranges from fine to coarse. That's because it is composed of intergrown crystals. The finer and more tightly interwoven the crystal components are, the better the jade.

Shape: The best quality jade is cut into cabochons. Ovals and rounds normally sell for more than rectangular, marquise and pear shapes. Smooth uncarved pieces are more valuable than carved ones. Carving allows the removal of flaws from inferior material.

Size: Since large, fine quality jadeite is rare, size does play a role in increasing its value. The thickness of good jadeite is also important. If a jadeite cabochon is thinner than 2mm or smaller than 8 x 6 mm, there can be a considerable deduction in its per-carat value.

Polish & Finish: The more brilliant the polish and the smoother the surface, the better the stone is. Every scratch, sharp angle and rough surface should be removed during the polishing process. When stones lose their luster and become scratched, they can be repolished. Texture and polish are related because fine-textured stones can take a higher polish than those with a coarse texture. Hardness is also important. Since nephrite is a little softer, it normally does not take as high of a polish as jadeite.

Jade Treatments

Waxing: This treatment is considered acceptable in the trade. It's commonly done after the final polish to improve luster and hide pits and cracks. The stone is soaked in a colorless molten wax and then buffed to achieve a good shine. Heat and strong solvents will undo this treatment. Material which has received only a superficial waxing is often called **A jade** in the trade.

Dyeing: This is often done to add green or lavender color to white or light-colored jade. The stone is heated to open up the "pores" and then dye is forced into it often with high pressure. Blueberry juice is a common dye for lavender jade. It looks good at first but it can fade in sunlight. Gemologists use a microscope and a spectroscope to detect dyes, but even with these instruments, dyes may be hard to detect. Dyed jade is called **C Jade**.

Heating: Dark green nephrite may be treated by this method to lighten the color of dark-green material. Red jade can be heated to increase redness, but the usual result is a dull brown, and transparency is reduced in the process.

Bleaching and polymer impregnation: This relatively new treatment removes brown from jade, making white colors whiter and green colors brighter. The jade is first soaked and bleached in chemicals. Microscopic tunnels are created as silica is removed during the process. Then the bleached jade is impregnated with a synthetic material to fill these tunnels. The resulting material is called **B jade**. Sometimes dye is used before impregnation and other times it is added to the filler. An article in the Fall 1992 issue of *Gems & Gemology* (pp. 176-187) discusses various tests for this treatment. The only definitive test is infrared spectroscopy, which requires sophisticated equipment that few gem labs have. Don't plan on handing bleached jade down to

Fig. J.8 An assortment of jadeite bangles and rings. Hinged bangles sell better in western countries, but all other factors being equal, they are less valued than one-piece bangles. The green and white jade in the one-piece bangle is referred to as "moss-in-snow." *Photo and jewelry courtesy Mason-Kay.*

Fig. J.9 Black nephrite and dark gray jadeite. *Courtesy Mason-Kay.*

Fig. J.10 Jadeite carving. If it were completely green, it would be worth more. If it were all lavender, it would be worth less. *Courtesy Mason-Kay.*

future generations; it will discolor with time and the tiny tunnels create durability problems. Prongs from mountings can dig into the "B jade," and dish-washing solutions and other substances can damage it over time. Sellers are supposed to disclose treatments, especially when they are not stable, but not all do.

When buying jade, deal with reputable jewelers. Ask how and if it has been treated. Have the treatment information written on the receipt. And have expensive pieces checked by major gem labs which have the experience and equipment required to test jade.

Colors of Jadeite and Nephrite

Green Jadeite: In good qualities, this is the most expensive jade. A very fine emerald-green cab (cabochon) that is translucent, evenly colored and 13 x 18mm can wholesale for over $20,000 if the color is natural. The same quality in a 6 x 8mm size might wholesale for over $2000. As the stones become more yellowish, grayish or less intensely colored, the price goes down. A very light grayish-green cab that is 6 x 8mm can sell for as little as $25.

Jadeite value is very much a function of how it is used. The way in which beads and cabs are valued illustrates this. A $10 green jadeite cab would normally be considered low quality. A $1000 strand of fifty 8mm green jadeite beads could be considered a nice example of jade jewelry. This strand would yield 100 cabs if the beads were cut in two, making the price of each cab $10. So material that produces decent beads makes substandard cabs.

Green Nephrite: Most nephrite is very affordable. The nephrite pendant and the pair of earrings shown in figure J.7 retail for less than $20 each. The antique value of old nephrite pieces often outweighs their intrinsic worth. Green nephrite is typically grayish, blackish or brownish. The more it approaches a pure green, the more desirable it is.

Lavender Jadeite: This jadeite can range in color from a light grayish-pink to a deep purple. A top-quality intense lavender cabochon that is 13 x 10mm may wholesale for over $2500.

"Red" Jade: Most so-called red jade is orange, brown or a rust-like brownish-red. This color is found on the outside of the rough and is presumably caused by the oxidation of the iron content from the surrounding water or earth. Jade pieces found in tombs can also look reddish-brown on the surface and along cracks penetrating the interior.

Black or Gray Jade: Black jade, which is mined in Wyoming and Australia, is usually nephrite. Gray jade is typically jadeite and can range from dark to light in color. Black and gray jade are relative new-comers to jade jewelry and have become quite popular in the past twenty years.

White jadeite: This can range from a translucent gray-white (water-jade) to an opaque, milky, white. Usually it's accompanied by other jade colors.

White Nephrite: Normally, this jade is not a true white. It's usually grayish. When it has a yellowish cast, it is sometimes referred to as **"mutton-fat" jade**. This jade is used to make attractive carvings.

For additional information, consult *Jade* by Roger Keverne, *Jade, Stone of Heaven* by Richard Gump, and *Jade for You* by John Ng and Edmond Root. The last two books are currently out of print but may be found in libraries or used bookstores.

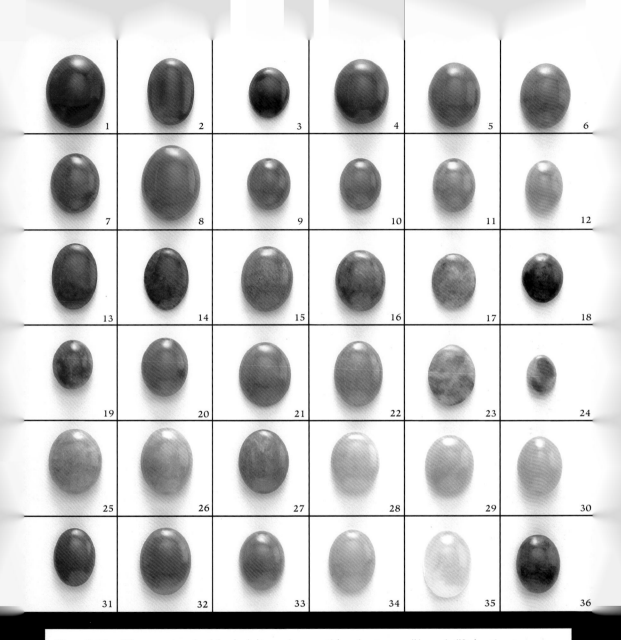

Fig. J.11 The most valuable jadeite cabs on this chart are #1 and #2 in the top row. Number 1 is the most expensive, even though #2 photographed better in the photo. The most valuable lavender cab is #25. In the bottom row, #31 is the most valuable color. Note: the actual colors of these stones may be slightly different than shown. The printing and developing processes usually alter the true color of gems in photographs. *Chart and stones courtesy Mason-Kay; photos by Richard Rubins.*

Lapis Lazuli (a rock composed of lazurite and some calcite, pyrite and other minerals)

9th wedding anniversary stone

For over 5000 years, lapis lazuli (lapis) has been mined in Northeastern Afghanistan. This is still the world's most important source both in terms of quality and quantity. During the 1980's, Afghan rebels sold a great deal of lapis in order to get cash for weapons. They used these against the Russian troops who invaded their country. As a result, the price of lapis dropped.

The name *lapis lazuli* is from the Latin word for stone, *lapis,* and the Persian *lazhward* meaning blue. Up until the Middle Ages, lapis was called *sapphirus*, which also means blue. In ancient texts such as the Bible, the term sapphire most likely refers to lapis lazuli.

The Ancient Egyptians, Greeks and Romans not only used lapis for adornment, they ground it up to make eye shadow, medicine and a pigment called ultramarine, which was used in many of the world's famous paintings. Today lapis is one of the most popular stones for men's jewelry and it is used to make beads, watch dials, boxes, figurines and other decorative articles.

The most valued lapis has a natural, even, deep violet-blue color that is free of white calcite veining. It also has a high polish and a bit of pyrite. Dyed lapis is the least valuable type. Dye is used to improve the color and to hide white calcite. Often, the dye is not very stable and may rub off on your skin. A wax coating is commonly used to seal in the dye and to make the polish look better. It's not always possible for a salesperson to know if lapis has been dyed. However, if they claim the color is natural and the stone is untreated, have them write this on the receipt. Generally, most lapis beads are dyed. Dye can frequently be detected by rubbing the stone with cotton dipped in finger-nail polish remover or alcohol. Never do this in a conspicuous spot and always get permission first.

The second most important source of lapis is Chile. However, Chilean lapis tends to contain a lot of white calcite and the color can be relatively light. Consequently it is often dyed. German and Swiss lapis are not lapis lazuli. They're blue dyed jasper, the most widely used lapis imitation.

Fig. L.1 Lapis lazuli. The cabochon with the teardrop shape has the best depth of color.

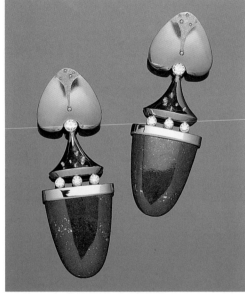

Fig. L.2 Lapis lazuli earrings made by Richard Kimball. *Photo by Steve Ramsey.*

Malachite (Cu₂CO₃OH₂) a hydrated copper carbonate; a common ore of copper

Malachite $(Cu_2CO_3OH_2)$ a hydrated copper carbonate; a common ore of copper

As early as 3000 BC, malachite was recovered from the copper mines of Egypt and Israel. Besides being used for jewelry, magic charms and ornaments, it was ground into powder and worn as eye make-up. The same powdered pigment is used by painters under the name of mountain green.

Malachite is usually banded with differing shades of green in agate-like patterns. It's beautiful, yet low-priced. You should be able to find, for example, a nice-quality 12 x 10 mm cabochon for less than $15. Reasonably-priced beads, figurines, mosaics, boxes and other decorative objects are also available. Often, malachite is banded and intermixed with other copper minerals such as blue azurite. In this case, the resulting material is called **azurmalachite**.

Due to its perfect cleavage and very low hardness (3.5 - 4), malachite can easily break and scratch. It's also sensitive to heat, acids and ammonia. Sometimes, malachite is impregnated with wax or epoxy to improve the polish and hide small cracks. Never clean it ultrasonically; just wipe it with lukewarm, soapy water and rinse.

Currently, Zaire is the major producer of malachite. Other sources include Russia, Zambia, Namibia, Arizona, New Mexico and Australia.

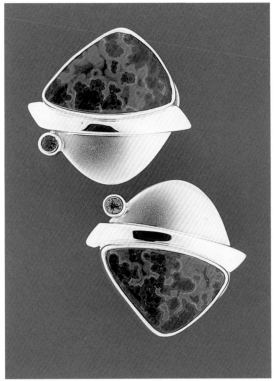

Fig. Ma.1 Azurmalachite earrings. *Design by Lori Braun; jewelry & photo copyright by Murphy Design.*

Fig. Ma.2 Malachite carving.

Moonstone & Some Other Feldspars (A group of closely related minerals)

Moonstone—Alternate birthstone for June

Over half of the earth's crust is composed of minerals from the feldspar group and most are not gemstones. All varieties require special care since they can be easily cleaved (split) and chipped. In fact, "feldspar" is derived from "field" and "spar," a word that refers to any shiny rock that cleaves easily. Listed below are optical and physical properties of feldspars.

Hardness	6 - 6.5	Optic Character	DR, biaxial, AGG reaction common
RI: 1.52 - 1.54 (moonstone & amazonite); 1.54 - 1.55 (oligoclase); 1.56 - 1.57 (labradorite)			
SG: 2.54 - 2.63 (moonstone & amazonite); 2.62 - 2.65 (oligoclase); 2.69 - 2.72 (labradorite)			
Crystal System: Monoclinic (moonstone); triclinic (amazonite, oligoclase and labradorite)			
Pleochroism: Usually none, but some transparent types may show weak to moderate pleochroism			
Cleavage: Perfect and easy in two directions; parting is also common			
Toughness: Poor; feldspars should not be cleaned in ultrasonics or with steamers			
Stability to heat: May crack or cleave; amazonite may also lose color			

MOONSTONE: In India, people once believed that moonstone was solidified moonlight. It is supposed to bring good fortune and help you foretell future events. Moonstones are noted for a floating light effect and sheen called **adularescence**, which has been compared to the light of the moon. This phenomenon results from alternating layers of two kinds of feldspar (usually orthoclase and albite) which cause light to scatter. High moonstone cabochons may resemble cat's-eye gems due to the concentration of light along the top of the stone.

Moonstone is typically white, colorless or light grayish blue, but it may also be yellow, orange, brown, blue or green. It ranges from near transparent to almost opaque. The most valued stones are blue and near transparent—sometimes $100 a carat. Translucent white stones can cost less than $5 per carat. Major sources are Sri Lanka, Burma and India.

LABRADORITE: This name most often refers to a dark, opaque feldspar, first found in Labrador, that displays a flash of color(s) when viewed at certain angles. This optical effect, called **labradorescence**, is typically bright blue, but it can also be green, yellow, orange or rarely purple. In a more general sense, "labradorite" includes some feldspars which are more transparent. Examples would be Oregon sunstone and **rainbow** labradorite, a nearly transparent, colorless stone with multicolored labradorescence. This labradorite is often sold as **rainbow moonstone**.

YELLOW ORTHOCLASE: A collector stone, this is usually transparent and faceted.

SUNSTONE: There are two main types of sunstone. The best known, aventurine feldspar (oligoclase), is opaque and has glittery red or golden inclusions. Another transparent type, labradorite, is orange, yellow, red or colorless. It is the state gem of Oregon.

AMAZONITE (Amazon Stone): A bluish-green variety, this is sometimes sold as "Pikes Peak jade" in Colorado. It's also found in Virginia, India, Russia and Africa.

Fig. Fe.1 Moonstone

Fig. Fe.2 Yellow orthoclase. *Photo Robert Weldon.*

Fig. Fe.4 Amazonite

Fig. Fe.3 Oligoclase sunstone

Fig. Fe.5 Labradorite sunstone. State gem of Oregon.

Fig. Fe.6 Labradorite

Fig. Fe.7 Rainbow labradorite

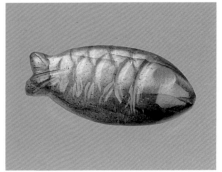

Fig. Fe.8 Carved labradorite fish

Opal

Opal SiO_2nH_2O—Silica + water, about 3 to 10% water in opals with a play-of-color
Alternate birthstone for October and 14th wedding anniversary stone

Before 1829, opals were said to bring good fortune because they possessed the colors and powers of all gemstones. Then Sir Walter Scott published his novel *Anne of Gerstein*. In it, one of the characters wore a gorgeous opal that would change color depending on her mood. One day when a few drops of holy water were sprinkled on the opal, she fainted and died shortly thereafter. Convinced that this meant opals were unlucky, readers stopped buying the gem. Within a year of the novel's publication, the opal market had crashed and prices were down about 50%. The fact that opals occasionally crack when cut and set reinforced this new superstition. Queen Victoria helped the stone regain its popularity. She wore it during her reign and she gave opal jewelry to her children and friends. Thanks to opal finds in Australia in the 1870's, the queen had a good selection to choose from.

The ancient Latin name for opal was *Opalus*, which was apparently derived from the Sanskrit *Upala* meaning "precious stone." The Greek word for opal, *opállios*, means "to see a change (of color)." White opal was probably first mined at Czerwenitza, Czechoslovakia (formerly Hungary). Archival evidence shows that this mine was in operation in the 14th century, but it most likely was worked much earlier. In Mexico, fire opal was probably known to the Aztecs as early as the 13th century. The first unrecorded discovery of opal in Australia is said to be in 1849; the 1872 discovery of boulder opal in Queensland was the first recorded find. Today the greatest proportion of the world's opal comes from Australia. Opal is also found in Mexico, Brazil, the U.S., Japan and Honduras, but the finest quality is produced in Australia.

If you were to examine opal under an electron microscope at 20,000X magnification, you would see a mass of closely packed, tiny silica spheres. Opals show a **play-of-color** (a shifting of spectral colors) when the spheres are of uniform size and arranged in regular three-dimensional layers. The color or range of colors of the opal are determined by the size of the spheres. Light bends and splits as it passes through the spheres, causing spectral colors to appear at different angles. The brighter and more distinctive the play-of-color, the better the opal. Not all opals show a play-of-color. However, they do share the following properties:

RI	1.44 - 1.47 Mexican opal: as low as 1.37, but usually 1.42 - 1.43	**Crystal System**	Mainly amorphous
SG	1.98 - 2.20	**Optic Character**	SR, ADR common
Hardness	5 1/2 - 6 1/2	**Cleavage**	None
Pleochroism	None	**Light Stability**	Stable

Reaction to Heat: Sudden temperature changes may cause opals to crack or craze. Over-heating can turn opals white or brownish and cause the play-of-color to disappear.

Toughness: Very poor to fair depending on source and type of opal. Dealers usually keep their opals for a period of time to verify they are not susceptible to crazing, a network of fine cracks.

Fig. Op.1 White opal pendant. *Design, cutting and photography by Paul B. Downing.*

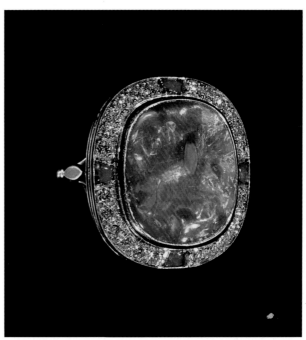

Fig. Op.2 An early 20th century, black opal ring. The intensity of the red is exceptional. *Courtesy Port Royal Antique Jewelry; photo by Harold & Erica Van Pelt.*

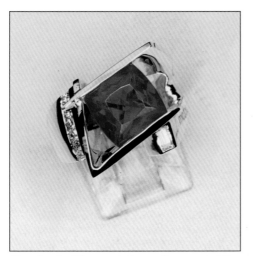

Fig. Op.3 Fire opal ring. *Courtesy of Rox Designs; photo by John Wallace.*

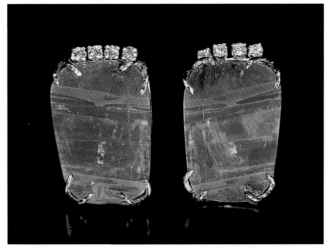

Fig. Op.4 Boulder opal earrings. These opals are worth more as a matched pair than if they were sold individually. *Port Royal Antique Jewelry; photo by Harold & Erica Van Pelt.*

Opal Varieties, Types and Trade Names

COMMON OPAL (POTCH): Opal with **no** play-of-color and a translucent to opaque transparency. It occurs in various body colors and is generally of little value. Opal with a play-of-color, the most popular kind, is called **precious opal** by many opal dealers. Red and orange Mexican opal is commonly called **fire opal** even if it has no play-of-color.

LIGHT OPAL (includes white opal, grey opal, crystal and jelly opal): Opal with a play-of-color and a light body color. **White opal** is the most common type. It typically has an off-white background color and can be translucent to opaque. Milky white stones with little play-of-color are used in budget-priced jewelry. White opals with a brilliant play-of-color can retail for a few hundred dollars per carat. When an opal has a high transparency, a near colorless body color and a distinct play-of-color, then it is called a **crystal opal**. This is the most valued light opal. In its highest qualities, it can cost more than $2500 a carat retail. A translucent opal with a play of color is sometimes called a **semi-crystal opal**. **Jelly opal** or **water opal** is near transparent to translucent and shows either an indistinct play-of-color or none at all. You can buy it for as little as $5 a carat. Better qualities may sell for $100 to $200 per carat.

BLACK (DARK) OPAL (includes black opal, semi-black opal, black crystal opal): "**Black opal**" is often used as a generic term for any opal which has a play-of-color against a dark background. In a more strict usage, black opals have a play-of-color against a black or very dark background. If the background is mid-gray to dark, the stone is classified as a **semi-black opal**. If the stone is translucent or semi-transparent and dark with a play-of-color, the stone is a **black crystal opal**.

The dividing lines between black, semi-black and gray opals can vary from one dealer to another. You need to look at comparison stones to understand the various depths of body colors and even then it can be hard to distinguish between some black and mid-black opals.

When black opal was discovered in Australia in 1903, it was not well accepted. Many people assumed that it was treated opal or white opal cemented to black onyx. Some jewelers considered it valueless. Today top-grade black opal can sell for $15,000 a carat. Some exceptional stones have even sold for over $20,000 a carat.

BOULDER OPAL: Opal that is still attached to the rock (usually ironstone) in which it is found. This opal is found in boulders whose cracks and spaces have been infiltrated with opal. Boulder opal, which can resemble either light or dark opal, is typically cut in irregular shapes. Fine quality boulder opal often sells for several thousand dollars per piece, but you can also get attractive stones for a few hundred dollars. For people who cannot afford a colorful black opal, boulder opal can be a good alternative. It costs less because the stone is not solid opal. It is a layer of opal naturally adhered to a rock backing.

MATRIX OPAL or **OPAL-IN-MATRIX:** Stones with lines or spots of opal randomly scattered (mixed) throughout the **matrix** (host rock—the rock in which a mineral, fossil or pebble is found). There are several types found in the market. The most common is a porous opal from Andamooka, Australia, which is often dyed black to simulate black opal. **Yowah opal**, another type of matrix opal, is completely natural and is mined in Yowah, South Queensland. The patches and lines of opal in its ironstone matrix often form distinctive patterns. Matrix opal normally sells for much less than boulder opal.

FIRE OPAL: A transparent to translucent opal with a red, orange, yellow or brownish body color both with or without a play-of-color. Mexico is the principle source. Since consumers often

Fig. Op.5 Colorful examples of common opal: Source, top left to right—Oregon, Africa, Nevada, Africa, Oregon; bottom left to right—Mexico, Oregon, Mexico, Mexico, Peru.

Fig. Op.6 Light-colored boulder opal pendant.

Fig. Op.7 Left to right: a crystal shell opal (ancient shell replaced by opal), a crystal opal from Lightning Ridge, and a semi-crystal opal.

Fig. Op.8 Yowah opal ring. *Rox Designs; photo by John Wallace.*

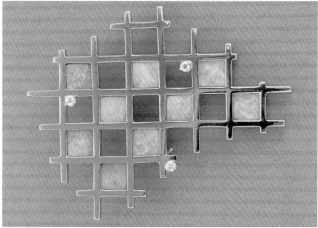

Fig. Op.9 White opal squares set in a brooch. *Designed, constructed and photographed by The Diamond Dove, Inc.*

assume that a fire opal is any opal with a lot of red play-of-color, some trade members think it would be better to simply call it orange or red opal, depending on its color. The most valued fire opal is reddish orange, transparent, and has a play-of-color within the stone. This quality can retail for as much as $300 per carat. Translucent stones that are yellowish or brownish may sell for around $5 per carat.

Treatments, Assembled Stones, Etc.

Opal is sometimes impregnated with oil, wax or plastic to improve the play-of-color and to prevent or disguise cracking. The plastic is stable, but the oil and wax isn't. There are various techniques for creating the appearance of black opal. These include smoke impregnation, backing with black or colored paint, and treatment with dye, silver nitrate or sugar carbonized by acid. One should avoid repolishing or applying solvents to treated opal.

If you'd like a stone with a black-opal look at an inexpensive price, consider getting an opal doublet or triplet. An **opal doublet** is a thin slice of opal cemented usually with black glue to another material such as potch opal, chalcedony or glass. If this doublet also has a protective top of colorless quartz or glass, then it is called an **opal triplet**. Doublets are normally more expensive than triplets because more opal is used. Do not confuse these assembled stones with boulder opal, which has a naturally attached backing. Often you can detect the man-made stones by looking at them from the side. A doublet typically has a straight separation line whereas a boulder opal has a crooked one. There are also fake opal stones. One is called **Slocum Stone** and another **Opalite**. Hong Kong is a major producer of imitation opal. Synthetic opal is grown in Japan and Russia.

Factors Which Affect Opal Value

Type of Opal: Solid black opal is more expensive than white or boulder opal if similar qualities of each category are compared. Matrix opals and assembled stones are the least expensive types. There's a great difference in price between a natural and an assembled opal of similar appearance, so it's important to have salespeople identify the type of opal both verbally and on the receipt.

Body Color (Base or Background Color): Black opal is more expensive than light opal of like quality. With black and boulder opal, generally the blacker the background color the more valuable the stone is. When determining base color, you must look at the top of the stone.

Brilliance: The overall brightness and intensity of the play-of-color. The more brilliant the flashes of color, the better the stone. Examine brilliance both under a consistent light source and away from it. Stones that maintain their brightness away from light are the most highly valued. Brilliance is one of the most important value factors.

Play-of-Color: The dominant color(s) and the combination of colors are both important. Intense red is the most rare and therefore the most prized color. In terms of value, it is followed by orange, green and blue, the most plentiful color. The way in which different color combinations are priced can vary from one dealer to another. Any type of play-of-color can be desirable, as long as the colors are intense and not dull when viewed face up.

Fig. Op.10 This distinctive black opal is called the "globe opal" because its patterns resemble the oceans and continents. *Courtesy Port Royal Antique Jewelry; photo by Harold & Erica Van Pelt.*

Fig. Op.11 A black opal with exceptional brilliance and a high intensity of color. Compare it to the opal in the preceding photo. *Port Royal Antique Jewelry; photo Harold & Erica Van Pelt.*

Fig. Op.12 Boulder opal with matrix showing. *Courtesy Proprioro; TKO Studios.*

Fig. Op.13 A black opal with a predominantly red color. This is a rare, collector-quality opal. *Port Royal Antique Jewelry; photo by Harold & Erica Van Pelt.*

Fig. Op.14 A low-quality milky white opal.

Fig. Op.15 Side view of an opal doublet.

Fig. Op.16 Face-up view of same doublet.

Color Pattern: The diffracted colors in opals are displayed in various patterns: **pinfire**—small pin-point like color specks; **flashfire**—larger splashes of color, usually irregular in shape; **broad flashfire**—sheets of color normally covering a large section or all of a stone's surface; **harlequin**—square or angular patches of color set close together like a mosaic; **fancy patterns and picture stones**—unusual patterns that form pictures or resemble things such as Chinese writing, straw, flowers, cat's-eye stones, etc. Pinfire and small type patterns are generally less desirable than broad patterns or large flashes. Harlequin and distinctive fancy patterns are especially valuable.

Transparency: For light opal and fire opal, the higher the transparency, the more valuable the stone. For black opal, the opaque, blacker stones tend to be more highly valued than those with greater transparency.

Shape: The most sought-after traditional shape is a well-formed oval. It tends to bring a higher price than other shapes because it's in greater demand, it's easier to set, and valuable opal material is sacrificed when stones are cut as ovals. Many jewelers and designers, however, prefer other shapes, especially freeforms because they are more distinctive. Unusual freeforms may sell for more than ovals, especially after they are mounted.

Cut: All else being equal, domed cabochons tend to be more valued than flat ones. Excessive weight on the bottom and a thin or unsymmetrical profile can all reduce the value of an opal.

Size and Carat Weight: Stones under a carat are generally worth less per carat than larger ones. If a stone is unusually large, it may be worth less per carat than stones more suitable for general jewelry use. Boulder opals are typically priced by size rather than carat weight. The larger the opal the higher the price.

Imperfections: Opal value decreases when there are eye-visible imperfections on the top of the stone such as sand or gypsum. The larger and more noticeable they are, the greater their impact on value. Inclusions on the back of a stone have little or no effect on price unless they hurt the structural integrity of the stone. Cracks drastically reduce value. A common opal flaw is **crazing**—a thin, network of fractures that resembles a spider web. When deep, it has a serious impact on price. Opals with a high water content are the ones most subject to crazing. There are ways of concealing crazing, but no honest opal dealer would do that without disclosing it. Many dealers offer some type of guarantee against crazing that is typically valid for one year. However, this guarantee is not against cracks, which are usually the result of abuse or poor setting skills. To prevent crazing in dry environments such as safe deposit boxes, some dealers store their opals in distilled water. Others say this is unnecessary. At any rate, water does not hurt the opal. Opals sometimes have pattern lines which look like cracks but aren't. These lines are natural changes in the pattern of an opal and are not regarded as flaws.

Since opals are relatively soft and fragile, they require special care. Avoid heat and sudden changes of temperature. Do not wear them while sunbathing or set them on a sunny window sill or under hot lights. Do not clean them in ultrasonics. Instead, wash them in lukewarm water with a mild soap and soft cloth. (Opal doublets and triplets, however, should not be immersed in water.) Store opal jewelry separately in cloth pouches. Take rings off when doing housework and engaging in sports. With proper care, opals can give you a lifetime of enjoyment.

Two good sources for more information on opal evaluation are *Australian Precious Opal* by Andrew Cody and *Opal Identification and Value* by Paul Downing.

Fig. Op.17 Pinfire pattern in a boulder opal pendant. *Port Royal Antique Jewelry; photo by Harold & Erica Van Pelt.*

Fig. Op.18 An unusual cat's eye pattern in a black opal. *Port Royal Antique Jewelry; photo by Harold & Erica Van Pelt.*

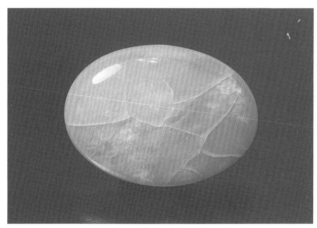

Fig. Op.19 A rare Australian black opal with a play of color that is mostly red, pink and orange. *Port Royal Antique Jewelry; photo by Harold & Erica Van Pelt.*

Fig. Op.20 A badly crazed white opal.

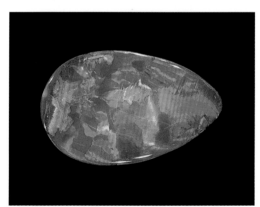

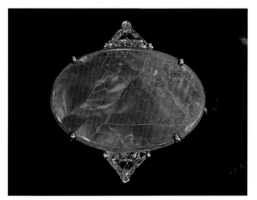

Fig. Op. 21 A black opal with a flashfire pattern and internal crazing. *Port Royal Antique Jewelry; photo by Harold & Erica Van Pelt.*

Fig. Op.22 This black opal sold at a low price because it looked cracked. It turned out that the opal simply had pattern lines. *Port Royal Antique Jewelry; photo by Harold & Erica Van Pelt.*

Peridot   (Olivine group, forsterite species) $(Mg,Fe)_2SiO_4$—Magnesium iron silicate

August birthstone, 16th wedding anniversary stone

According to legend, you will be protected from evil spirits if you wear peridot (also called **chrysolite**).   This rich, yellowish-green gem has sometimes been mistaken for emerald.   Many of Cleopatra's "emeralds" were probably peridots.   Adding further confusion, peridot was called topaz in ancient times.

Peridot is attractive, yet affordable.   You can purchase a high quality peridot for less than $250 per carat retail.   The greener the stone and the better the clarity, the higher the value is.   If yellow or orange colors complement your skin, then peridot jewelry should also look good on you.   It is particularly flattering to people with blond or red hair.

Peridot has been mined for over 3500 years.   The oldest source is St. John's Island, Egypt, in the Red Sea.   Pakistan and Arizona are the main sources today.   Other deposits include Myanmar, China, Brazil, Kenya and Norway.   Physical and optical characteristics of peridot are given below:

RI	1.64 - 1.69	**Crystal System**	Orthorhombic
SG	3.27 - 3.45	**Optic Character**	DR, biaxial + or -
Hardness	6 1/2 - 7	**Cleavage**	Indistinct
Toughness	Fair to good	**Pleochroism**	Weak
Stability to Heat: Rapid or uneven heat can cause peridot to crack or break.			
Reaction to Chemicals: Attacked by sulfuric and HCl acid. Acid perspiration of some people over a long period may etch the surface. Jewelers should never put peridot in pickling solutions.			

Fig. P.1 Peridot and freshwater pearl pendant

Fig. P.2 Peridot ring hand-crafted by Varna Platinum

118

Spodumene   LiAlSi$_2$O$_6$—Lithium and aluminum silicate

KUNZITE, which is pink to purple in color, is the best-known spodumene variety. Found in California in 1902, it was named after George Frederick Kunz, a famous gemologist and former vice-president of Tiffany & Co. Some of the kunzite available today is irradiated to intensify its color. Unfortunately, the color fades over time when exposed to strong light or heat. Kunzite is typically eye-clean and low priced. You can find well-cut, light pink stones of high clarity for under $100 per carat retail. Stones with a more saturated color are available, but they can be difficult to find in North America or Europe. These stones are often reserved for buyers in Japan.

Spodumene can also be yellow to green in color. The rare emerald-green variety is called **HIDDENITE**. It was discovered in North Carolina in 1879 by William Hidden. Don't expect to find hiddenite in your local jewelry store or rock shop. The deposit is very small and production has always been sporadic. In 1904, mineralogist Max Bauer valued fine, green transparent hiddenite at $50 to $100 per carat in his book, *Precious Stones*. According to mineralogist John S. White, the North Carolina site is currently being worked, and a deep-green, 1-carat hiddenite from there is now priced at about $10,000. Some light green material from Brazil and other areas is sold as hiddenite. However, many gemologists feel it should technically be called green spodumene. They also believe that irradiated green stones do not merit being called hiddenite.

The major sources of kunzite and other spodumene varieties are Afghanistan, Brazil, Madagascar and the U.S. Physical and optical characteristics of spodumene are given below:

RI	1.66 - 1.68	**Crystal System**	Monoclinic
SG	3.14 - 3.21	**Optic Character**	DR, biaxial positive
Hardness	6 1/2 - 7	**Cleavage**	Perfect in two directions
Toughness	Poor	**Pleochroism**	Moderate to strong trichroism
Reaction to heat: Sensitive; kunzite fades; irradiated green spodumene fades rapidly.			
Stability to light: Kunzite fades; irradiated green spodumene fades rapidly			

Fig. Sp.1 Green spodumene crystal

Fig. Sp.2 Kunzite

Ruby & Sapphire (Corundum) Al_2O_3—Aluminum Oxide

Ruby—July birthstone; sapphire—September birthstone; ruby—15th & 40th anniversary stone; sapphire—5th & 45th anniversary stone

Ruby and sapphire have a lot in common. They are the same mineral—corundum. They have the same physical characteristics. They have both been considered regal and sacred. In ancient India, the ruby was called the "king of gems." In England the ruby was used for coronation rings. Sapphires were worn by kings and queens for good luck and they were set in rings for bishops and cardinals. Their blue color symbolized heaven. The ancient Hindus thought that if they offered a ruby to the god Krishna, they would be reborn as an emperor.

Color is what distinguishes ruby from sapphire. Rubies are red and sapphires are either blue or another color such as green, orange, pink, yellow, purple, colorless or black (sapphire colors other than blue are called **fancy colors)**. It wasn't until about 1800 that ruby and sapphire were recognized as being the same mineral. Before then, red spinel and garnet were also called ruby. The name was derived from the Latin word for red, *rubeus*. "Sapphire" is from a Greek word meaning blue.

Rubies and sapphires are harder than all other gems except diamonds. Their superior hardness combined with the lack of cleavage makes them a very durable gem. It also makes them valuable for industrial purposes. They have been produced synthetically so they can serve as laser windows, tips in ball-point pins, styluses for record players and jewel bearings in watches, meters and aircraft instruments. The properties of ruby and sapphire are given below.

RI	1.76 - 1.78	Crystal System	Trigonal
SG	3.95 - 4.05	Optic Character	DR, uniaxial negative
Hardness	9	Cleavage	None, twinned stones may show parting

Toughness: Excellent except for fractured or repeatedly twinned stones; over-heated stones may abrade easily.

Pleochroism: Ruby, strong purplish red and orangy red; sapphire, moderate to strong violetish blue and greenish blue; fancy-color sapphires, weak to strong dichroism

Stability to Light: Stable except for irradiated yellow and orange sapphires, which may fade

Varieties

RUBY: In 1896, German mineralogist Max Bauer wrote: *A clear transparent, and faultless ruby of a uniform deep red colour is at the present time the most valuable stone known.* Today diamonds have surpassed rubies in value, but Bauer's description of a top-quality ruby is still valid. Dealers disagree, however, on whether orangy-red rubies are better than those which are purplish-red. They would agree that a strong red fluorescence is desirable and that top-grade stones should have a minimal amount of black, gray or brown. Their color should also look good in any light. The highest percentage of stones that have met these color criteria are from Myanmar (Burma), which is currently a major source of ruby. Do not assume, though, that a ruby is good quality if it originates from Myanmar. Likewise, do not assume that rubies from

120

Fig. RS.1 Above: Sapphire and diamond necklace. *Photo and necklace courtesy Harry Winston, Inc.*

Fig. RS.2 Right: Thai ruby and diamond ring. *Photo and ring courtesy Color Masters Gem Corp.*

other localities such as Thailand, Cambodia, Vietnam, Tanzania and Kenya must be inferior. High-quality material has originated from all of these countries.

Large rubies have sold for as much as $200,000 per carat, but good rubies with inclusions in the 1-carat range are available for $3000-$4000 per carat. You can also find opaque rubies for as low as $10 per carat. A premium may be charged if a high-grade stone originates from Myanmar or shows no evidence of heat treatment, providing it has a lab report from a respected lab. Rubies are commonly heat-treated to improve color and/or clarity. Diffusion treatment, large glass fillings and red oils or dyes greatly affect value (see chapter on treatments).

SAPPHIRE: When used by itself, the term **sapphire** normally refers to the blue variety. In its highest qualities, it is more expensive than the other varieties. Top-quality Kashmir sapphires, for example, can wholesale for over $15,000 a carat (Mining in Kashmir has been extremely limited for decades). There are differences of opinion as to what is the best sapphire hue. Some say blue, others say violetish blue. Most dealers agree, however, that greenish blues are less valuable. Dealers also have different tone preferences. Some prefer medium tones of blue while others prefer medium-dark tones. Pale, blackish or grayish stones, however, cost the least. Good sapphires in the one-carat range are available for $1000 to $2000 retail. Kashmir sapphires have the highest prestige, followed by those from Burma and then Sri Lanka. Other big producers of sapphire are Thailand, Cambodia and Australia. The lowest priced stones often come from Australia because they tend to be overly dark and have a low transparency. Sapphire is also found in India, Montana, China and various African countries. Sapphires are usually heat treated. Their outer surface is sometimes darkened by diffusion treatment, but this must always be disclosed.

PADPARADSCHA: A pinkish-orange sapphire, padparadscha is the rarest and most prized of all the fancy sapphires. Its name is believed to have come from the Sinhalese word for the lotus flower, which has a similar color. Frequently, orange sapphire is called padparadscha, but most corundum dealers agree that both pink and orange hues must be present for a stone to be a true padparadscha. Don't expect to find this rare gem at your local jeweler's.

PINK SAPPHIRE: Next to the padparadscha, this is the most highly prized of all the fancy sapphires. Since "pink" is a synonym of "light red" and since fine rubies cost more than sapphires, many Asian dealers prefer to call pink sapphires rubies. The jewelry trade in western countries prefers to treat the pink sapphire as a unique stone with its own merits, rather than as a second-rate ruby. High-quality pink sapphires can cost several thousand dollars per carat.

ORANGE, PURPLE, YELLOW OR GREEN SAPPHIRE: East Africa, Sri Lanka, Thailand and Montana are sources of these sapphires. A high percentage of green sapphire is found in Australia. Of these four sapphire colors, orange is the most valued; green is typically the lowest priced; and yellow is usually the most readily available.

COLORLESS SAPPHIRE (WHITE SAPPHIRE): In recent years, this sapphire has become popular as a diamond substitute. Unlike cubic zirconia, it is a natural gemstone.

STAR SAPPHIRE AND STAR RUBY: Star corundum with a fine blue or red color is rare. Gray, maroon and black star stones are easier to find, and their prices can be relatively low.

More detailed information on the identification and quality analysis of corundum is available in *The Ruby & Sapphire Buying Guide* by Renée Newman and in *Corundum* by Richard Hughes (his newest edition is entitled *Ruby & Sapphire*).

Fig. RS.3 Sapphires come in a wide range colors, as this photo shows. The dividing line between ruby and pink sapphire or reddish orange sapphire is debatable. Three of the stones pictured would be called rubies by many dealers. Others would call them sapphires. In Asia, even the two light pink stones might be identified as sapphires. *Gemstones courtesy Cynthia Renée Co; photo by Robert Weldon.*

Fig. RS.4 Star sapphire (6.80 cts). It's unusual to find a natural blue star sapphire with such a distinct and well-centered star. *Photo courtesy Asian Institute of Gemological Sciences (AIGS)*

Fig. RS.5 Padparadscha. *Gemstone courtesy Radiance International; photo by Robert Weldon.*

MgAl$_2$O$_4$—Magnesium aluminum oxide

22nd wedding anniversary stone

If you're looking for a natural gem that resembles a ruby but costs a lot less, you should consider getting a spinel. It's durable, comparatively hard and typically has a better clarity and brilliance than a ruby. Not all red spinels can pass as rubies, but many do. Some of the world's largest and most famous "rubies" are really spinels, such as the "Black Prince's Ruby" and the 361-ct "Timur Ruby" in the English crown jewels. Spinel comes in other colors such as blue, pink, orange and black, but red is the most valued. Stones over ten carats are rare.

Natural spinel does not enjoy the popularity that it merits. One reason for this is that it's often confused with the synthetic spinel used in inexpensive birthstone rings and costume jewelry. In addition, natural spinel is not available in mass quantities, so it's not widely known and advertised. However, custom jewelers and collectors who like unusual gems appreciate spinel.

The main sources of spinel are Myanmar (Burma) and Sri Lanka. Other localities include Thailand, Cambodia, Afghanistan, Tanzania, Russia and Vietnam. Spinel is often a by-product of the search for ruby and sapphire. Its properties are as follows:

RI	1.71 - 1.73 (gem spinel)	Crystal System	Cubic
SG	3.57 - 3.63 (black spinel, up to 4.0)	Optic Character	SR
Hardness	8	Cleavage	Poorly developed
Toughness	Good	Pleochroism	None
Stability to Light: Stable			

Varieties

RED SPINEL: The most valuable red spinels resemble a high-quality ruby. A one-carat stone can retail for over $2500. Low-quality brownish stones are available for under $100 a carat.

PINK SPINEL: This resembles pink sapphire but costs about 1/4 to 1/2 the price.

ORANGE SPINEL: Its color range is from yellow-orange to red-orange. This spinel is sometimes called **flame spinel**. Formerly it was called **rubicelle**.

BLUE SPINEL: Fine blue colors are rare and can retail for over $2000 per carat. This spinel tends to be grayish or very dark. In an attempt to lighten the color, stones are often cut shallow. Blue spinel is mined in Sri Lanka and Myanmar.

BLACK SPINEL: This spinel is opaque and rarely seen in jewelry.

COLOR-CHANGE SPINEL: A rare stone, it's grayish-blue in daylight and purplish under incandescent light-bulbs.

STAR SPINEL: This is rare and generally gray, blue or black with 4 or 6 rays.

Fig. S.1 A very rare and fine 10.68-ct Tanzanian pink spinel. *Gem from Cynthia Renée Co.; ring by Paul Klecka; photo by Robert Weldon.*

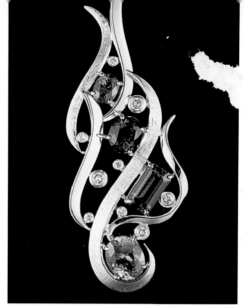

Fig. S.2 Spinels in a pendant by Gary Dulac. *Photo copyright 1994 by Azad.*

Fig. S.3 Burmese red spinel and spinel crystals. *Gems from Cynthia Renée Co; photo by Robert Weldon.*

Fig. S.4 Spinel ring created and photographed by LInda Quinn.

Fig. S.5 Blue spinel ring from Cynthia Renée Co. *Photo by Robert Weldon.*

Tanzanite & Other Zoisites Ca$_3$Al$_3$(SiO$_4$)$_3$(OH)—Calcium aluminum hydroxysilicate

Tanzanite—24th wedding anniversary stone

No history, lore or poetry was needed for tanzanite to become one of the most popular gems on the market. You just look at it and fall in love with it. From one angle it may display a rich blue color, from another it can look purple. Along with the blue and purple, there may be flashes of red, green, yellow, orange or brown. What's more, tanzanite can appear one color indoors and another outdoors. A high clarity and transparency add to its beauty.

Tanzanite was discovered in the 1960's in the foothills of Africa's Mt. Kilimanjaro. Later, Henry Platt, vice-president and director of Tiffany's, named the stone after its country of origin, Tanzania. Some mineralogists feel that the term "tanzanite" should be restricted to transparent zoisites that range in color from blue to violet to purple in color. Other colors such as green, yellow and pink are to be called by their mineralogical name **zoisite**. But since "tanzanite" sounds more exotic and appealing, some dealers tend to use it for all transparent zoisites. However, as with sapphire, the unmodified "tanzanite" refers to the blue or violet variety, whereas other colors must be specified, e.g. yellow tanzanite. This practice allows dealers to distinguish between the transparent and non-transparent green varieties. In the marketplace, for example, green tanzanite is transparent green zoisite whereas green zoisite is typically the non-transparent variety used for carvings. Some European mineralogists call the green, non-transparent type, **anyolite**. Listed below are the properties of zoisite.

RI	1.69 - 1.70	Crystal System	Orthorhombic
SG	3.20 - 3.40	Optic Character	DR, biaxial positive
Hardness	6 - 7	Cleavage	Perfect in one direction
Toughness: Poor to fair; tanzanite's perfect cleavage makes it vulnerable to bumps and knocks.			
Pleochroism: Very strong; in tanzanite, the trichroism is blue, purple and green, yellow or brown.			
Reaction to Chemicals: Attacked by hydrochloric and hydrofluoric acid			
Stability to Light: Stable; the colors resulting from heat treatment are permanent.			

TANZANITE: Some dealers feel that a deep blue with a faint purple secondary color is the most desirable. Others prefer an equal mix of blue and purple. Most dealers would agree, though, that blue stones are worth more than those which are purple. Light lavender stones are priced the lowest. You can find high-quality, deep-blue tanzanite with purple overtones for less than $1000 per carat retail. Attractive light lavender tanzanite is available for less than $300 per carat retail. Most tanzanite is heat-treated to intensify the color and/or eliminate brown, gray or green. For more information on tanzanite, consult the *Emerald & Tanzanite Buying Guide* by Renée Newman.

THULITE: This semi-translucent pink zoisite, often mottled with gray, is used for cabochons or carvings. Also called **rosaline**, thulite is found in Norway, Austria, Italy, Australia and the U.S.

GREEN, YELLOW, ORANGE or PINK TRANSPARENT ZOISITE: It may be hard to find these varieties. Their prices are usually in the same range as those of blue or purple tanzanite.

GREEN ZOISITE: Often found with ruby, this translucent to opaque zoisite is frequently carved.

Fig. Tz.1 Five zoisites viewed under incandescent light bulbs. It's unusual for a tanzanite to remain as blue as the one in the upper right-hand corner in this type of lighting. It would normally become purplish.

Fig. Tz.2 Green zoisite carving

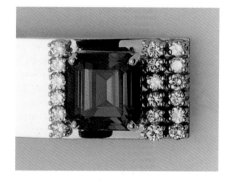

Center right: **Fig. Tz.3** Tanzanite. *Jewelry and photo from Robert Trisko Jewelry Sculptures.*

Bottom right: **Fig. Tz.4** Tanzanite ring by Proprioro. *Photo by TKO Studios.*

Topaz   Al$_2$(F,OH)$_2$SiO4—aluminum fluorohydroxysilicate

November birthstone, imperial topaz—23rd wedding anniversary stone

Most topaz is light brown when mined and then turns colorless after exposure to light or low heat. Otherwise it tends to be pale blue. That's why yellow, orange and pink topaz are highly regarded. Good brilliance and hardness also add to their value. High-quality, yellow-orange topaz, for example, may cost several hundred dollars per carat whereas citrine quartz of similar color and quality may sell for less than $35 a carat. Due to the price difference, some sellers call citrine quartz, which is widely available, "quartz topaz" or even "topaz" to make it sound more expensive. Prior to the 18th century, all yellow stones and some green ones were usually called "topaz." Even today, some miners refer to almost any yellow stone as a topaz. Therefore, when buying topaz, ask the seller to specify on the receipt that it is genuine topaz and not quartz or another gemstone.

The world's largest producer of topaz is the state of Minas Gerais in Brazil. For almost 300 years, its Ouro Preto district has supplied the world with yellow, orange and pink topaz. Other sources include the U.S., Pakistan, Sri Lanka, Russia, Germany, Mexico, Australia and Myanmar. Crystals weighing several kilos are common. The properties of topaz are as follows:

RI	1.61 - 1.64	Crystal System	Orthorhombic
SG	3.50 - 3.57	Optic Character	DR, biaxial positive
Hardness	8	Cleavage	Perfect in one direction

Toughness: Poor. Due to its perfect cleavage, stones can easily break, chip or form straight cracks when dropped or knocked. Topaz requires special care when being set.

Pleochroism: Weak to distinct trichroism

Stability to light: Natural brownish topaz may fade, especially some from Mexico, Utah and Siberia. Yellow non-irradiated stones from Brazil and pink or blue ones are generally stable.

Varieties

PINK to RED TOPAZ: Top-grade red or strong pink topaz is the most valuable type of topaz. The redder and more saturated the color, the rarer and more costly the stone. Natural-color stones, which generally come from Pakistan, can sell for much more than those which are treated. Most pink topaz is heated brownish-yellow topaz from Brazil.

GOLDEN YELLOW to ORANGE TOPAZ: When this variety is intensely colored and has reddish or pink overtones, it is called **imperial topaz** and can retail from about $200 to over $2000 per carat. Stones that lack pink highlights or have a low color saturation are less valuable.

BLUE to GREEN TOPAZ: Produced by irradiating and then heating certain colorless material, blue topaz can look like fine aquamarine, but most is a stronger blue and looks less natural. Ever since the market was flooded with this topaz, its price has dropped to levels below $20 a carat.

COLORLESS TOPAZ: Used to simulate diamonds, this is the cheapest and most plentiful topaz.

Fig. Tp.1 Blue topaz pendant created and photographed by Linda Quinn

Fig. Tp.2 Suite of imperial topaz from Cynthia Renée Co. *Photo by Robert Weldon.*

Fig. Tp. 3 Imperial topaz ring by Cheri Del Santo. *Topaz from Cynthia Renée Co.; photo by Robert Weldon.*

Fig. Tp.4 Pink topaz. *Stone from Manoel Bernardes Ltd. Photo by Robert Weldon.*

Fig. Tp. 5 Colorless topaz with an unusual inclusion

Fig. Tp.6 Brown topaz. The color-zoned stone on the left is light brown, colorless and gray.

Tourmaline (a group of mineral species)

Alternate birthstone for October and 8th wedding anniversary stone

No other gemstone offers buyers a wider variety of colors than tourmaline. Besides being found in every color of the rainbow, tourmaline may also be multicolored in one piece.

It wasn't until the early 18th century that tourmaline was recognized as a distinct gemstone. Up to that time, the red and green varieties were often classified as a type of ruby or emerald. Then it was discovered that tourmaline possessed curious properties. When heated or pressed at one end, it became electrically charged; it could attract and repel light-weight, non-metallic materials like ashes, dust and small bits of paper. In 1768, Linnaeus, a Swedish naturalist, suggested that green tourmaline was related to **schorl**, the black species of tourmaline which had been known for almost two centuries in Europe. The origin of "tourmaline" is uncertain. According to *Gems* by Robert Webster, it originated from the Sinhalese *turmali*, a name applied by the local jewelers to yellow zircon. Supposedly, a parcel of tourmaline was sent by mistake under this name to stone dealers in Amsterdam in 1703, and the name may have stuck.

Tourmaline has been found in significant quantities in Brazil, California, Maine, Pakistan, Afghanistan, East Africa, Madagascar, Sri Lanka and the Soviet Union. Its properties are below:

RI	1.62 - 1.65	Crystal System	Hexagonal (Trigonal)
SG	3.00 - 3.26	Optic Character	DR, uniaxial negative
Hardness	7 - 7½	Cleavage	None

Toughness: Fair; heat-treated stones may be more fragile than untreated stones
Pleochroism: Moderate to strong, usually light and dark tones of the same body color
Reaction to Heat: Sudden temperature changes can cause fracturing. Strong heat may cause irradiated stones to fade.
Stability to Light: Normally stable, but some irradiated stones may fade with prolonged exposure.

Varieties and Species:

GREEN TOURMALINE: This variety is plentiful and comes in a wide range of shades. It tends to have a strong green dichroism that makes one direction of the stone (the optic axis) appear very dark and non-transparent. To lighten and improve the color, green tourmaline is commonly heat-treated. Stones that are brownish, blackish and yellowish are the least expensive. Those with an intense green color resembling a good emerald cost the most.

Top-color green tourmalines are found in East Africa and are typically colored by chromium. As a result, they are called **chrome tourmalines**. Not all stones sold as "chrome tourmaline" contain chromium. To test for chromium content, some dealers look at the tourmaline through a special color filter called a Chelsea filter. The stone will look reddish or pinkish instead of green if it contains chromium. Eye-clean green tourmaline is readily available. Therefore, good-quality stones are expected to have a high clarity. Top quality chrome tourmaline can *wholesale* for as much as $1000 per carat. Most green tourmaline, however, is quite affordable, with retail prices ranging from about $20 in very low qualities to $400 per carat in better stones.

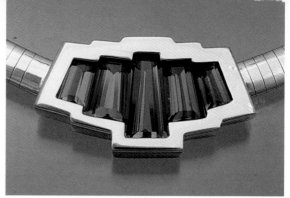

Fig. Tm.1 Indicolite ring by Richard Kimball. *Photo by Steve Ramsey.*

Fig. Tm.2 Green-tourmaline slide pedant made and photographed by Linda Quinn

Fig. Tm.3 Red tourmaline ring by Richard Kimball. *Photo by Steve Ramsey.*

Fig. Tm.4 Well-matched bi-color tourmaline ring & cuff-links. *Jewelry by Cynthia Renée Co.; photo Robert Weldon*

Fig. Tm.5 Carved portrait in a slice of a watermelon tourmaline crystal.

Fig. Tm.6 Black tourmaline (schorl)

PINK or RED TOURMALINE: The discovery of pink tourmaline in southern California in 1898 helped popularize this stone. Red and pink tourmaline are also mined in Afghanistan, Brazil, Africa and Madagascar. **RUBELLITE** is a trade name applied to tourmaline that is red in both daylight and incandescent light. (Tourmalines that are red often turn brownish under incandescent light bulbs, and this is undesirable.) Many sellers apply the term "rubellite" to any tourmaline that is strong pink or red. But no matter which name is used, tourmalines that are pink or that look brownish-red under incandescent light should sell for less than pure-red rubellites, all other factors being equal. True-red rubellites tend to have a low clarity. A higher clarity should be expected of brownish red or very light pink tourmalines. Clean, pure-red rubellites can wholesale for over $2000 per carat.

Pink and red tourmalines are commonly irradiated to intensify their color. The stones are not radioactive and the color is relatively stable. However, strong heat like that from a display window or a jeweler's torch can cause the color to fade. The color will return if the stone is irradiated again. Sometimes rubellite is treated with fillers to improve its clarity. Even when treated, you should expect it to have a lower clarity than other transparent tourmalines.

BLUE TOURMALINE (INDICOLITE or INDIGOLITE): Indicolite comes in various shades of blue, but frequently, it's a dark greenish or grayish blue. The color is often lightened with heat treatment. A brighter turquoise-blue material has been found in Northeastern Brazil in the state of Paraíba. It's called **Paraíba tourmaline** and is the rarest and most expensive tourmaline. In its finest qualities, it has wholesaled for up to $10,000 a carat. Paraíba tourmaline can also have an intense green or violet color. Don't expect to find it in your local jewelry store; it's rare and highly coveted. Indicolite costs less, ranging in price from about $100 to $800 retail per carat.

YELLOW, ORANGE, BROWN or GOLDEN TOURMALINE: Yellow and orange tourmaline occur naturally but are sometimes produced by irradiating light yellow or green tourmaline. Heat can cause the resulting color to fade. The orange and yellow stones may retail for about $30 to $350 per carat. Brown tourmaline, tends to be less expensive.

COLORLESS OR WHITE TOURMALINE: This tourmaline occurs naturally in the same areas as pink tourmaline. It can also be produced by heating light pink tourmaline.

BLACK TOURMALINE (Mineralogical name **SCHORL**): This is a very common opaque stone which was widely used for mourning jewelry during the Victorian era in Britain. Today it's occasionally used instead of jet or chalcedony in very inexpensive jewelry.

BICOLORED or MULTICOLORED TOURMALINE: The pink and green variety is the most common type, but stones can also be pink and colorless or blue and green. Some stones have more than two colors. The most valued stones have distinct saturated colors with sharp boundaries and no fractures. Green and pink slices of crystal tourmaline that have concentric color banding are called **watermelon tourmaline**.

CAT'S-EYE TOURMALINE: This is found in a variety of colors but pink and green are less difficult to find than red or blue colors. Cat's-eye tourmaline is occasionally treated with epoxy fillers to improve transparency and seal the tubes causing the cat's-eye. The fillers prevent dirt from entering the tubes. Retail prices range from about $30 to $700 per carat.

COLOR-CHANGE TOURMALINE: In daylight, this tourmaline may look yellowish to brownish green whereas under incandescent light it appears orangy red. Color-change tourmaline is rare and considered a collector's item.

Fig. Tm.7 Pink tourmaline crystal. *Pendant by Dan Miller; photo by Luciano Baldi.*

Fig. Tm.8 Paraiba tourmaline leaf pendant by Gary Dulac. *Photo copyright 1994 Azad.*

Fig. Tm.9 Cat's-eye tourmalines

Fig. Tm.10 Blue-green tourmaline with red tourmaline side stones. *Jewelry by Cynthia Renée Co.; photo by Robert Weldon.*

Fig. Tm.11 Pinkish-orange tourmaline ring created and photographed by Linda Quinn.

Turquoise $CuAl_6(PO_4)_4(OH)8 \cdot 5H_2O$—hydrated copper aluminum phosphate

December birthstone and 11th wedding anniversary stone

If you go on a tour of Arizona or New Mexico, you'll no doubt see Indians selling turquoise jewelry. On the back of it, there may be a stamp saying "Made in Taiwan." Unfortunately, a glut of cheap turquoise jewelry has lowered the prestige and value of what was for centuries a highly esteemed gem. Turquoise was admired by the ancient Egyptians for its distinctive color. It is the national gemstone of Iran (Persia), where it has decorated thrones and the attire of high officials. In Tibet, it has had a role comparable to that of jade in China. To the Aztecs, turquoise was a commodity more valuable than gold. According to the 17th century book *Gemmarum et Lapidum Historia* by Anselmus de Boot, turquoise was so highly regarded by European men, that no man considered his hand to be well adorned unless he wore a fine turquoise.

The best turquoise occurs in northeast Iran near Nishapur, where it has been mined for over 3000 years. The material there is typically more stable and blue than that of other sources—China, Mexico, the Sinai Peninsula and Southwestern USA, the main producer. Persian turquoise made its way to Europe via Turkey, which is probably why by the 13th century, the French were calling it *pierre turquoise—Turkish stone*. The properties of turquoise are given below:

RI	1.61-1.65	Crystal System	Triclinic
SG	Usually 2.60 - 2.85	Optic Character	AGG (DR)
Hardness	5 - 6	Cleavage	None
Toughness	Poor to good	Pleochroism	Weak
Reaction to Heat: Can fracture, shatter, crackle and discolor			
Stability to Light: Untreated material may fade or discolor			
Reaction to Chemicals: May be discolored by perspiration, perfume, hair-spray, cosmetics, lotions, heavy liquids, soap and ultrasonic cleaning solutions. It dissolves very slowly in HCL.			

As this chart shows, natural turquoise has stability problems. If it is not from Iran and it is not treated, it may turn green, white or occasionally brown within a year after it is mined. Porous material can crack or crumble. This is why almost all of the turquoise sold today has been treated—usually with a plastic substance designed to prevent discoloration and increase durability. A colorant may be added to improve the color. Sometimes turquoise is impregnated with wax to deepen the color and decrease porosity. However, the wax can pick up dirt and gradually discolor. When buying turquoise, assume it has been treated unless you are dealing with a knowledgeable, trustworthy seller who writes on the receipt "untreated natural turquoise."

The most highly valued turquoise is untreated and dense and has an even, intense sky-blue color. Usually, this type of material is from Iran. The value is reduced if the color is green or pale or if inclusions or lines called "spider-webbing" are present. Some people, though, prefer greenish colors and patterned turquoise. Prices can range from $1 a stone to a few hundred dollars for a top-quality, untreated cabochon. In the 1970's, the same cab might have sold for $2000. Turquoise in genuine Indian jewelry or antique pieces may be worth a lot more than loose stones of the same quality.

Fig. Tq.1 Chinese turquoise beads and a carving of untreated turquoise from the Sleeping Beauty Mine in Globe, Arizona. This mine is noted for producing high-quality turquoise.

Fig. Tq.2 Turquoise earrings created by Richard Kimball. *Photo by Steve Ramsey.*

Fig. Tq.3 Turquoise bracelet purchased from Indians in Arizona. The inscription "Navaho by John Silversmith" is found on the back.

Zircon ZrSiO$_4$—Zirconium silicate

December birthstone

Zircon is not the same as cubic zirconia (CZ). Zircon is a natural gemstone with exceptional brilliance and a diamond-like luster. Cubic zirconia is a synthetic stone with a different chemical composition. When colorless and well-cut, both stones resemble diamonds. Before CZ was introduced to the market in 1976, heat-treated, colorless zircon was widely used as a diamond imitation. As a result, many people mistakenly think zircon is just a fake stone.

Zircon comes in almost every color of the spectrum. Today, most zircon sold in jewelry stores is blue. This color results from heating brownish zircon. Before the 1900's, orange or reddish-brown zircon, called **hyacinth**, was the most common type. The name "zircon" may have originated from the Persian word *zargun* meaning gold-color. Three of the main sources of zircon are Cambodia, Thailand and Sri Lanka. It is also found in Vietnam, Myanmar, Tanzania, France and Australia. Bangkok is the world's cutting and marketing center for zircon.

There is a wide variation of properties among zircons so mineralogists classify them into at least two types: those with low properties and those with high ones (RI above ≈ 1.90, specific gravity above ≈ 4.6, and a hardness of $\approx 7\ 1/2$). Some zircons may be classified as an intermediate type. Zircon property ranges are given below:

RI	1.78 - 2.01	Crystal System	Tetragonal
SG	3.9 - 4.8	Optic Character	DR, Uniaxial positive
Hardness	6 - 7 1/2	Cleavage	Imperfect & negligible
Toughness: Untreated stones—fair to good; heated stones—poor to fair, chip and abrade easily			
Pleochroism: Weak to moderate except in blue stones, where it's strong blue and brownish yellow to colorless.			
Stability to Light: Some heat-treated stones may revert to their original color.			

Varieties

BLUE ZIRCON: It often resembles aquamarine and blue topaz but has more fire and brilliance. The blue zircon sold in jewelry stores is heat treated and susceptible to abrasions, especially when mounted in rings. Retail prices can range from $20 to $500 per carat.

GREEN ZIRCON: Found mostly in Sri Lanka, this zircon is often grayish or yellowish. It's not uncommon for street vendors to sell it as green tourmaline or green sapphire. A curious property of green zircon is that it usually emits some level of natural radioactivity.

YELLOW, ORANGE & BROWN-RED ZIRCON: In their natural state, these zircons tend to be either brownish or pale. Heat treatment can intensify the color and reduce brown tints. To verify the colors are stable, dealers sometimes expose them for several days to the sun.

COLORLESS ZIRCON: This variety occurs rarely in nature, but can be produced by heating brownish zircon. Today, CZ has replaced colorless zircon as the most popular diamond imitation.

Fig. Z.1 Zircon rings by Nanz Aalund. *Gems from Cynthia Renée Co.; photo by Robert Weldon.*

Fig. Z.2 Blue zircon earrings from Timeless Gem Designs

Center right: **Fig. Z.3** Three different colored zircons from Overland Gems

Bottom right: **Fig. Z.4** Unheated zircon from Cynthia Renée Co. *Photo by Robert Weldon.*

12

Caring for your Gems

Cars, furniture and clothing will look better and last longer if you take care of them. The same is true of gems. Clothing manufacturers sew written instructions into their products. They'll say, for example, "dry clean only," "no bleach," "cool iron," etc. It's not possible to place this kind of information on gems. Therefore, you must rely on salespeople, brochures and books for instructions on how to look after your gem and jewelry purchases.

It's important to realize that colored gemstones are not as durable as diamonds. Diamonds are used as drills, they're boiled in acid, they're heated and then plunged in water. Don't treat colored gems in this manner. Many gems are very susceptible to **thermal shock**—sudden temperature changes. These include emerald, garnet, kunzite, opal, peridot, quartz, tanzanite, topaz and tourmaline. You should not, for example, lay in the sun and then jump in a swimming pool while wearing these gems, nor should you go from a hot oven to a cold sink of water or from a hot tub to a cold shower. If you do, the sudden temperature change could possibly cause the stones to crack or shatter.

With some stones, you should avoid heat in general. These include amethyst, emerald, kunzite, malachite, opal, red tourmaline and turquoise. Don't leave these gems sitting on a sunny window sill or wear them to the beach. The heat might make amethyst, kunzite and red tourmaline fade and it could dry out and discolor the fillings in emerald. It could cause small cracks in some malachite, opal and turquoise.

Malachite and turquoise are unusually sensitive to chemicals. Ammonia and acid solutions as well as everyday products such as perfumes and lotions can harm them. Pickling solutions used by jewelers and some acids will etch the surface of peridot. Solvents such as alcohol and acetone will gradually dissolve the fillers in emeralds and other oiled or filled stones. Dyed lapis, dyed jade and other dyed stones are also adversely affected by solvents. Chlorine can gradually pit and dissolve gold alloys. The pitting can also occur while swimming or while soaking in a hot tub with chlorine.

The safest way to clean a gemstone is to wash it in lukewarm water using a mild liquid soap or detergent that contains no ammonia. Then dry it with a soft, lint-free cloth. If the dirt can't be washed off with a cloth, try using a toothpick or a Water Pik to remove it. If that doesn't work, have it professionally cleaned. Jewelers often clean stones with ultrasonic cleaners, which send high frequency sound waves through solutions. The vibrating fluid removes built-up dirt, but it can also shake poorly-set stones from their mountings and damage some types of gems. The table on the next page indicates which stones should not be cleaned in ultrasonics. Most of the data in the chart is from the GIA *Gem Reference Guide*, an article by Deborah Martin in the summer 1987 issue of *Gems and Gemology* entitled "Gemstone Durability: Design to Display," and an article by Howard Rubin entitled "Jewelers' Guide to Gemstone Handling."

Gemstone	Ultrasonic, safe?	Comments
Aquamarine	Use caution	
Chalcedony	Use caution	Chemicals may attack dyed stones
Chrysoberyl	Usually safe	
Diamond	Usually safe	Ammonia, acids and repeated ultrasonic cleaning may damage some fracture fillings
Emerald	Avoid	Avoid heat and solvents like acetone and alcohol
Garnet	Use caution	Avoid thermal shock; ultrasonics are risky if liquid inclusions are present
Iolite	Risky	Avoid acids and thermal shock
Jade	Usually safe	Acids can affect polish on stones. Avoid solvents and ultrasonics if dyed.
Kunzite	Avoid	Avoid heat and strong light to prevent fading
Lapis Lazuli	Avoid	Avoid acids, acetone and other solvents
Malachite	Avoid	Avoid chemicals and heat
Moonstone	Avoid	Avoid heat
Opal	Avoid	Avoid thermal shock
Peridot	Use caution	Avoid acids and pickling solutions
Quartz	Use caution	Avoid thermal shock
Transparent Ruby & Sapphire	Use caution	
Star Ruby & Sapphire	Risky	Avoid ultrasonics with black star sapphires and with oiled or dyed stones
Spinel	Usually safe	
Tanzanite	Avoid	Avoid thermal shock
Topaz	Avoid	Avoid thermal shock
Tourmaline	Risky	Avoid thermal shock
Turquoise	Avoid	Avoid heat and chemicals
Zircon	Risky	Avoid thermal shock

Ultrasonic cleaners should also be avoided with:

♦ Badly flawed stones of any species—they can be further damaged by ultrasonic cleaning.

♦ Oiled and/or dyed stones—the oil and dye may be removed, often quickly.

♦ Stones with glass-filled cavities—the filling may fall out.

♦ Any kind of fracture-filled stone, including diamond. The cleaning solution or vibration could cause the fillings to gradually cloud, discolor or be removed.

You may be wondering why the preceding table says to use caution when cleaning certain gems in ultrasonic cleaners. These gems are sometimes likely to have inclusions that weaken the stone, but it's usually safe to clean them ultrasonically.

Some stones are more susceptible to knocks and bumps than others. This is because of their easy cleavage (ability to split along certain crystal planes). Kunzite, tanzanite, iolite, topaz and feldspars such as moonstone and sunstone all fit in this category. If these gems are knocked lightly just right at a specific angle against a wall or furniture, they can sometimes crack. Diamonds also cleave, but it normally takes a hard blow or lots of pressure to create diamond cleavage. So don't assume that a tanzanite or a topaz can withstand the same abuse as a diamond. You must treat them with much more care.

The most durable colored stones are jade, ruby, sapphire, chrysoberyl and spinel. Jade is softer than many gems, but its toughness (resistance to chipping, breaking and cracking) surpasses all other gem materials, including diamond. The other stones listed in the table can also provide good wear. Just treat them as you would a fine silk scarf or any other accessory.

Storing Your Jewelry

When you store jewelry, protection from theft and damage should be a prime consideration. A jewelry box can protect pieces from damage if they are stored individually, but it is one of the first places burglars look when they break into a home. So it's best to reserve jewelry boxes for costume jewelry when they are displayed on tables or dressers.

Jewelry pieces should be wrapped separately in soft material or placed individually in pouches or the pockets of padded jewelry bags. If a piece is placed next to or on top of other jewelry, the metal mountings or the stones can get scratched. Use your imagination to find a secure place in your house to hide jewelry pouches, bags and boxes. If expensive jewelry is seldom worn, it's best to keep it in a safe deposit box.

Miscellaneous Tips

♦ Avoid wearing jewelry (especially rings) while participating in contact sports or doing housework, gardening, repairs, etc. In fact, it's a good idea to take most colored-stone jewelry off when you come home and change into casual clothes. If during rough work you want to wear a ring for sentimental reasons or to avoid losing it, wear protective gloves. However, even gloves won't offer full protection.

◆ Occasionally check your jewelry for loose stones. Shake it or tap it lightly with your forefinger while holding it next to your ear. If you hear the stones rattle or click, have a jeweler tighten the prongs.

◆ Don't remove rings by pulling on any of their gemstones. Instead grasp the metal ring portion. This will help prevent the stones from coming loose and getting dirty.

◆ When you set jewelry near a sink, make sure the drains are plugged or that the piece is put in a protective container or on a spindle. Otherwise, don't take the jewelry off.

◆ Take a photo of your jewelry (a macro lens is helpful). Just lay it all together on a table for the photo. If the jewelry is ever lost or stolen, you'll have documentation to help you remember and prove what you had.

◆ Clean your jewelry on a regular basis. Once a week is not too often for a ring that is worn daily. Risky cleaning procedures can be avoided by regular cleaning.

◆ About every six months, have a jewelry professional check your ring for loose stones or wear on the mounting. Many stores will do this free of charge, and they'll be happy to answer your questions regarding gem care. Jewelers want you to enjoy the jewelry you purchase from them. You will. Just treasure it and take good care of it.

Bibliography

Books and Booklets

Arem, Joel. *Color Encyclopedia of Gemstones*. New York: Chapman & Hall, 1987.

Bauer, Jaroslav & Bouska, Vladimir. *Pierres Precieuses et Pierres Fines*. Paris: Bordas, 1985.

Bauer, Dr. Max. *Precious Stones*. New York: Dover Publications, 1968.

Beesley, C. R. *Gemstone Training Manual*. American Gemological Laboratories.

Carmona, Charles. *Complete Handbook of Weight Estimation*. Pre-publication copy. To be published in 1998.

Ciprani, Curzio & Borelli, Alessandro. *Simon & Schuster's Guide to Gems and Precious Stones*. New York: Simon and Schuster, 1986.

Cody, Andrew. *Australian Precious Opal*. Melbourne: Andrew Cody Party Ltd., 1991.

Downing, Paul. *Opal Identification and Value*. Estes Park. Colorado: Majestic Press, 1992.

Federman, David & Hammid, Tino. *Consumer Guide to Colored Gemstones*. Shawnee Mission, KS: Modern Jeweler, 1989.

Gemological Institute of America. *Gem Reference Guide*. Santa Monica, CA: GIA, 1988.
Gemological Institute of America, *The GIA Diamond Dictionary, Third Edition*. Santa Monica, CA: GIA, 1993.

Geolat, Patti, Van Northrup, C., Federman, David. *The Professional's Guide to Jewelry Insurance Appraising*. Lincolnshire, IL: Vance Publishing Corporation, 1994.

Gump, Richard. *Jade Stone of Heaven*. Garden City, NY: Doubleday, 1962.

Gubelin, Eduard J. & Koivula, John I. *Photoatlas of Inclusions in Gemstones*. Zurich: ABC Edition, 1986.

Hall, Cally. *Gemstones*, Eyewitness Handbooks. London: Dorling Kindersley, 1994.

Hoover, D B. *Topaz*. Oxford: Butterworth-Heinemann Ltd, 1992.

Hughes, Richard W. *Corundum*. London: Butterworth-Heinemann, 1990

Jewelers of America. *The Gemstone Enhancement Manual*. New York: Jewelers of America, 1990-94.

Jewell, Bill. *The Buying Guide to Black Opals*. North South Wales: Mineral Resources, 1996.

Keller, Peter. *Gemstones of East Africa*. Phoenix: Geoscience Press Inc., 1992.

Kraus, Edward H. & Slawson, Chester B. *Gems & Gem Minerals*. New York: McGraw-Hill, 1947.

Kunz, George Frederick. *The Curious Lore of Precious Stones*. New York: Bell, 1989.
Kunz, George Frederick. *Gems & Precious Stones of North America*. New York: Dover, 1968.

Liddicoat, Richard T. *Handbook of Gem Identification*. Santa Monica, CA: GIA, 1981.

...rcum, David. *Fine Gems and Jewelry.* Homewood, IL: Dow Jones-Irwin, 1986.

Matlins, Antoinette L. & Bonanno, A. *Jewelry & Gems: The Buying Guide.* South Woodstock, VT: Gemstone Press, 1987.

Miller, Anna M. *Gems and Jewelry Appraising.* New York: Van Nostrand Reinhold Company, 1988.

Mumme, I. A. *The Emerald.* Port Hacking, N.S.W.: Mumme Publications, 1982.

Nassau, Kurt. *Gems Made by Man.* Santa Monica, CA: Gemological Institute of America, 1980.
Nassau, Kurt. *Gemstone Enhancement, Second Edition.* London: Butterworths, 1994.

Newman, Renée. *Diamond Ring Buying Guide, 5th Edition.* Los Angeles: Intl. Jewelry Publications, 1996.
Newman, Renée. *Emerald & Tanzanite Buying Guide.* Los Angeles: Intl. Jewelry Publications, 1996.
Newman, Renée. *The Ruby & Sapphire Buying Guide.* Los Angeles: Intl. Jewelry Publications, 1994.

O'Donoghue, Michael. *Identifying Man-made Gems.* London: N.A.G. Press, 1983.

O'Leary, Barrie. *A Field Guide to Australian Opals.* E. Malvern, Australia: Gemcraft Publications, 1984.

Pough, Frederick. *Rocks & Minerals.* Boston: Houghton Mifflin, 1983.

Ramsey, John L. & Ramsey, Laura J. *The Gem Collector's Handbook.* Seattle: Boa Vista Press, 1995.

Read, Peter G. *Gemmology.* Butterworth Heinemann, 1991,

Rouse, John D. *Garnet.* London: Butterworths, 1986.

Rubin, Howard. *Grading & Pricing with GemDialogue.* New York: GemDialogue Marketing Co., 1986.

Schumann, Walter. *Gemstones of the World.* New York: Sterling, 1977.

Schwartz, Dietmar. *Esmeraldas, Inclusoes em Gemas.* Ouro Preto, Brazil. Federal University of Ouro Preto, 1987.

Sinkankas, John. *Emerald and other Beryls.* Prescott, AZ: Geoscience Press, 1989.
Sinkankas, John. *Gemstone & Mineral Data Book.* Prescott, Arizona: Geoscience Press, 1988.

Sinkankas, John and Read, Peter. *Beryl.* London: Butterworths. 1986.

Sevdermish, M. & Mashiah, A. *The Dealer's Book of Gems and Diamonds.* Israel: Mada Avanim Yekarot Ltd., 1996.

Sofianides, Anna & Harlow, George. *Gems & Crystals from the American Museum of Natural History.* New York: Simon & Schuster, 1990.

Suwa, Yasukazu. *Gemstones Quality & Value* (English Edition). Gemological Institute of America and Suwa & Son, Inc., 1994.

Walters, Raymond. *The Power of Gemstones.* Chartwell Books, 1996.

Webster, Robert. *Gems, Fourth Edition.* London: Butterworths, 1983.

White, John S. *The Smithsonian Treasury Minerals and Gems.* Washington D.C.: Smithsonian Institution Press, 1991.

Woodward, Christine & Harding, Roger. *Gemstones.* New York: Sterling Publishing Co. 1988.

Wykoff, Gerald L. *Beyond the Glitter.* Washington DC: Adamas, 1982.

Zucker, Benjamin. *How to Buy & Sell Gems: Everyone's Guide to Rubies, Sapphires, Emeralds & Diamonds.* New York: Times Books, 1979.

Periodicals

Auction Market Resource for Gems & Jewelry. P. O. Box 7683 Rego Park, NY. 11374.

Australian Gemmologist. Brisbane: Gemmological Association of Australia

Canadian Gemmologist. Toronto: Canadian Gemmological Association.

Colored Stone. Devon, PA: *Lapidary Journal* Inc.

GAA Market Monitor Precious Gem Appraisal/Buying Guide. Pittsburgh, PA: GAA.

Gem. Radnor, PA: Chilton Publishing Co.

Gems and Gemology. Santa Monica, CA: Gemological Institute of America.

Gem & Jewellery News. London. Gemmological Association and Gem Testing Laboratory of Great Britain.

Gemstone Price Reports. Brussels: Ubige S.P.R.L.

The Guide. Chicago: Gemworld International, Inc.

Lapidary Journal. Devon, PA: *Lapidary Journal* Inc.

JewelSiam. Bangkok, Thailand.

Jewelers Circular Keystone. Radnor, PA: Chilton Publishing Co.

Jewelers' Quarterly Magazine. Sonoma, CA.

Journal of Gemmology, London: Gemmological Association and Gem Testing Laboratory of Great Britain.

Michelsen Gemstone Index. Pompano Beach, FL: Gem Spectrum.

Modern Jeweler. Lincolnshire, IL: Vance Publishing Inc.

National Jeweler. New York: Gralla Publications.

Palmieri's GAA Market Monitor. Pittsburgh, PA:

Rock & Gem. Ventura, CA: Miller Magazines, Inc.

Miscellaneous: Courses, notes, and leaflets

Gemological Institute of America Appraisal Seminar handbook.

Gemological Institute of America Gem Identification Course.

Gemological Institute of America Colored Stone Grading Course.

Gemological Institute of America Colored Stone Grading Course Charts, 1984 & 1989.

Gemological Institute of America Colored Stones Course. 1980 & 1989 editions.

Gemological Institute of America Jewelry Sales Course.

Jewelers of America. *A Guide to What You Should Know About Colored Gemstones*.

Rubin, Howard. "The Effects of Lighting on Gemstone Colors."

Rubin, Howard. "Jewelers Guide to Gemstone Handling." Rego Park, NY: GemDialogue Systems, Inc.

Index

Order Form

To: International Jewelry Publications
P.O. Box 13384
Los Angeles, CA 90013-0384 USA

Please send me:

_____ copies of the **GEMSTONE BUYING GUIDE**

_____ copies of the **EMERALD & TANZANITE BUYING GUIDE**

_____ copies of the **GOLD JEWELRY BUYING GUIDE**

_____ copies of the **PEARL BUYING GUIDE**

_____ copies of the **RUBY & SAPPHIRE BUYING GUIDE**

_____ copies of **VOIR CLAIR DANS LES DIAMANTS**
(French edition of the *Diamond Ring Buying Guide*)

Within California $21.60 each (includes sales tax)   _____

All other destinations $19.95 US each   _____

_____ copies of the **DIAMOND RING BUYING GUIDE** (English edition)

Within California $16.18 each (includes sales tax)   _____

All other destinations $14.95 US each   _____

Postage & Handling for Books

USA: first book $1.75, each additional copy $.75   _____
Canada & foreign - surface mail: first book $2.50, ea. addl. $1.50   _____
Canada & Mexico - airmail: first book $5.00, ea. addl. $3.00   _____
All other foreign destinations - airmail: first book $11.00, ea. addl. $6.00   _____

Total Amount Enclosed   _____
(Check or money order in USA funds)

Ship to:

Name_____

Address_____

City_____ State or Province _____

Postal or Zip Code_____ Country _____

Diamond Ring Buying Guide

"Filled with useful information, drawings, pictures, and short quizzes. . . presents helpful suggestions on detecting diamond imitations, in addition to well-though-out discussions of diamond cutting, and how the various factors can influence value . . . a very readable way for the first-time diamond buyer to get acquainted with the often intimidating subject of purchasing a diamond."
    Stephen C. Hofer, President, Colored Diamond Laboratory Services, *Jewelers' Circular Keystone*

140 pages, 73 color and 36 black/white photos, 7" X 9", $14.95 US

Ruby & Sapphire Buying Guide

"Solid, informative and comprehensive . . . dissects each aspect of ruby and sapphire value in detail and quizzes the reader on key points at the end of each chapter. . . a wealth of grading information . . . *The Ruby & Sapphire Buying Guide* is a definite thumbs-up for both the unskilled and semiskilled buyer and seller. There is something here for everyone."
    C. R. Beesley, President, American Gemological Laboratories. *Jewelers' Circular Keystone*

"Well-written—not so technical that you would need a dictionary to understand what is written and, most important, the information in it is all pertinent to anyone who wants to buy and sell colored gemstones. I have recommended this book to all my students and I enthusiastically recommend it to anyone interested in colored gemstones. Well done!"
    H. B. Leith, teacher-gemologist, master goldsmith

204 pages, 40 color and 85 black/white photos, 7" by 9", $19.95 US.

Gold Jewelry Buying Guide

A how-to manual on judging jewelry craftsmanship and testing gold, plus practical information on gold chains, Black Hills gold, gold-coin jewelry and nugget jewelry.

"This book should be required reading for consumers and jewelers alike! It offers step-by-step instructions for how to examine and judge the quality of craftsmanship and materials even if you know nothing about jewelry. Packed with close-up photos to demonstrate what is right and what is not, this book clears up all the doubts and misconceptions one might have. If you are thinking of buying, making or selling jewelry as a hobby, as a career or just one time, then this book is a great place to start."
    Alan Revere, master goldsmith and director of the Revere Academy of Jewelry Arts

172 pages, 35 color and 97 black/white photos, 7" by 9", $19.95 US.

AVAILABLE AT bookstores, jewelry supply stores, the GIA and the *Lapidary Journal* Book Club or by mail: See reverse side for order form.

Order Form

To: International Jewelry Publications
P.O. Box 13384
Los Angeles, CA 90013-0384 USA

Please send me:

_____ copies of the **GEMSTONE BUYING GUIDE**

_____ copies of the **EMERALD & TANZANITE BUYING GUIDE**

_____ copies of the **GOLD JEWELRY BUYING GUIDE**

_____ copies of the **PEARL BUYING GUIDE**

_____ copies of the **RUBY & SAPPHIRE BUYING GUIDE**

_____ copies of **VOIR CLAIR DANS LES DIAMANTS**
(French edition of the *Diamond Ring Buying Guide*)

Within California $21.60 each (includes sales tax)   _____

All other destinations $19.95 US each   _____

_____ copies of the **DIAMOND RING BUYING GUIDE** (English edition)

Within California $16.18 each (includes sales tax)   _____

All other destinations $14.95 US each   _____

Postage & Handling for Books

USA: first book $1.75, each additional copy $.75
Canada & foreign - surface mail: first book $2.50, ea. addl. $1.50   _____
Canada & Mexico - airmail: first book $5.00, ea. addl. $3.00   _____
All other foreign destinations - airmail: first book $11.00, ea. addl. $6.00   _____

Total Amount Enclosed   _____
(Check or money order in USA funds)

Ship to:

Name_____

Address_____

City_____ State or Province_____

Postal or Zip Code_____ Country _____